CW01187836

I Live
in Michael Hartnett

ag cuimhneamh as Béarla
ag taibhreamh as Gaeilge

thinking in English
dreaming in Irish

I Live
in Michael Hartnett

Edited by
James Lawlor

R

A REVIVAL POETRY BOOK

Revival Press
Limerick - Ireland

Revival Press is the poetry imprint of
The Limerick Writers' Centre
12 Barrington Street, Limerick, Ireland

www.limerickwriterscentre.com

First published 2013

Selection © Revival Press 2013
Poems © Individual authors plus Gallery Press
The rights of the above mentioned have been asserted

Cover Design: Jason Cooke
Book Design: Kelly Richards Printing Ltd.

Managing Editor: Dominic Taylor

ISBN: 978-0-9569092-2-0

A CIP record for this title is available from the British Library

All rights reserved. No part of this publication may be reproduced or transmitted in any form or by any means, electronic or mechanical without permission in writing from the publisher, except by a reviewer who may quote brief passages in a review.

I Live in Michael Hartnett is a joint initiative of Limerick Writers' Centre & Limerick County Council Arts Office.

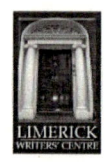

Limerick County Council
Comhairle Chontae Luimnigh

Contents

Foreword
Introduction

13	Eavan Boland	*Irish Poetry*
14	Carol Rumens	*Gift Birds for a Poet's Christening*
15	Peter Fallon	*End*
16	Mark Whelan	*Barn*
17	Dónal O'Siodhachain	*Hartnett Remembered*
18	John Liddy	*O Winged Bird*
19	Rita Kelly	*Missing You*
20	Augustus Young	*Sleeping Rough: After Rimbaud*
21	Tony Curtis	*The Flock*
23	Gerard Smyth	*Homage to Hartnett*
24	Pádraig J. Daly	*Ó hAirtnéide*
25	Mike Mac Domhnaill	*Michael Hartnett, File*
26	Mike Mac Domhnaill	*The Poet Hartnett*
27	Desmond Egan	*A Rhyme for Michael*
28	Eleanor Hooker	*In-sight of you*
29	Siobhán Campbell	*I was born in a will o the wisp*
30	Nuala Ní Chonchúir	*An tIasc - The Fish*
31	Gabriel Fitzmaurice	*So What If There's No Happy Ending?*
32	Declan Collinge	*Adharca Broic*
33	Louise Hegarty	*Between*
34	Doiréann Ní Ghríofa	*Féinphortráid ag Brionglóideach*
35	Rody Gorman	*Prioba-nan-Sùl*
36	Gerry Lyne	*For Michael Hartnett*
40	Pat Boran	*The Princess of Sorrows*
41	Huib Fens	*Templeglantine*
42	Brendan Kennelly	*In a Corner of O'Neills*
43	Valerie Sirr	*Hartstown Haiku*
44	Oliver Dunne	*M.H*
45	Paul Ó Colmáin	*Epilogue*
46	Liam O'Meara	*From Golden Hell, A Dream*
47	Teri Murray	*Saint Michael's Estate*
48	Mae Leonard	*That Night in Tallaght*
49	Eileen Casey	*Willow Man*
50	Mark Roper	*Curlew Sandpiper in the...*
51	Joe Healy	*Letter to Michael, August 2008*
53	Michael Coady	*Twenty-Four Hours from Tulla*
56	Tony Curtis	*The Garden Flat*
57	Aaron Smith	*Death of an Ulsterwoman*

58	Cathy Bryant	*Death of an Irishman*
59	Tom Matthews	*In Memoriam Michael Hartnett*
60	Catherine Phil MacCarthy	*Móin na nGé*
61	Ciaran O'Rourke	*Black Swans*
62	Carol Rumens	*The Elementalist*
63	Hayden Murphy	*Closing the Ears*
64	Eiléan Ní Chuilleanáin	*Michael and the Angel*
66	Michael O'Flanagan	*Resurrection*
67	Fred Johnston	*Flesh and Bone*
68	Donal O'Flynn	*In Memory of M.H. and Grandma*
69	B. D. Macmahon	*Four Meta-Haiku*
70	Eibhlín Nic Eochaidh	*Incommunicado*
71	Marian Finan Hewitt	*Seedling*
72	Paddy Bushe	*Final Version*
73	Greg Delanty	*Life*
74	Leland Bardwell	*"The Act of Poetry is a Rebel Act"*
75	Joe Horgan	*After Reading Michael Hartnett*
76	Seán Dunne	*Eoghan Rua on his Deathbed*
77	Christopher Murray	*A Farewell to Hartnett*
78	Pauline Fayne	*The Visit*
79	Catríona Ní Chléirchín	*Níl sa Saol ach...*
81	Robyn Rowland	*Éigse Michael Hartnett 2002*
82	Leonard Holman	*Listen*
83	Gréagóir Ó Dúill	*Samhailteacha de Mhícheál*
85	Macdara Woods	*West Going West*
87	Derry O'Sullivan	*Oidhreacht Mhichíl*
88	Michael Longley	*An October Sun*
89	Hugh McFadden	*Nine Mays Later*
90	Theo Dorgan	*Michael Michael*
91	Paul Durcan	*Michael Hartnett, The Poet King*
92	Anthony Croinin	*Remembering Michael*
93	Michael Coady	*Adhlacadh an Dreoilín*
94	Martin Vaughan	*Hartnett Abú*
95	John W. Sexton	*The True Poet Beckons Forever*
96	Carmel Cummins	*Ceist agus freagra éigin na teanga*
97	Gearoid O'Brien	*The Legacy of a Poet*
98	John Pinschmidt	*'After life's fitful fever...'*
99	Seamus Heaney	*Hartnett Laudation*
100	Paula Meehan	*Hagiography*

Foreword

There is a sense for me as I read through the poems in this collection *I Live in Michael Hartnett,* of the book almost writing itself. From the day the news broke on the 13th October 1999 that Michael Hartnett had died, his fellow poets have tried to capture in language and lyric, their sense of personal loss and the loss to literature of one of our greatest and much loved poets of the twentieth century.

The book while almost writing itself has been a long time in gestation. It was first mooted to me or more precisely a similar type book by poet and friend of Michael Hartnett's Theo Dorgan. For various reasons, mainly to do with resources, I didn't undertake it. So when Dominic Taylor of The Limerick Writers' Centre approached me in late 2011 resurrecting the idea again, the door was ajar. The door was pushed wide open when he suggested James Lawlor as editor. James is a young man from West Limerick, I knew him as a Hartnett scholar and enthusiast and that the book was now in safe hands. I would like to thank James and Dominic for their hard work and their steadfast approach in taking the original idea to this 'book in hand'.

The title *I Live in Michael Hartnett* we have taken with kind permission from Paula Meehan's poem Hagiography. It is apt, capturing the vibrancy of Hartnett's legacy on poets and poetry to this day and evident in the number of contributions to this collection. I would like to thank the contributors for generously allowing us include their work in this anthology.

The poems in *I Live in Michael Hartnett* range in sentiment including sadness, loss, regard, warm memories and humour. I was particularly heartened by the closing lines from Paul Durcan's poem 'Michael Hartnett, The Poet King' in which he says about Hartnett's life and passing "Forty years ago he would have been glad to know that forty years later he would gladly, not sadly die."

I Live in Michael Hartnett is the first anthology of poetry in celebration of Michael Hartnett. It will not be the last. To paraphrase, rather poignantly Michael Hartnett's own words from 'Death of an Irishwoman', "We loved him from the day he died".

Joan Mac Kernan
Limerick County Arts Officer
April 2013

Introduction

'I am a catalyst. But I'm a Roman catalyst'
Michael Hartnett

On the 13th September 1962, a week before his 21st birthday, Michael Hartnett left Newcastle West for a new life in Dublin. His mission was to escape the mundane and establish himself as a poet on the national scene. A few weeks previous, Professor John Jordan of University College Dublin had contacted him and offered him a scholarship to study at the institution. The professor would also publish three of Michael's poems in Poetry Ireland, which would ultimately announce his arrival on the national arena. Michael gladly left his life as a postman in Newcastle West, an existence he described as "hell" in a letter to the professor[1]. It would be the beginning of an unusual if not controversial career for a working-class man, who up to the age of twenty had never left Munster.

Within the decade Michael would travel around Europe and to parts of Africa, and would spend time in a Spanish jail for publicly reciting the poetry of Federico García Lorca. Michael's journey would have an internal dimension also, leading him into dark spaces within himself that he would struggle to escape. An outcome perhaps pre-empted in one of his very early poems 'Sad Singing in Darkness'[2] in which he wrote "Sad singing in darkness is our burden / for we have none to look to or to love. / We are lovers of rare earth; our plots / are few but flourish in the sunless angles." This sunless landscape would ultimately haunt and in some ways overcome him. This is all too clear in another one of Michael's poem's 'Sibelius in Silence'[3], where the speaker leaves the "friendly inns" and walks into the dark and happens upon a "calvary of signposts / on which strange names were shown / that pointed out the way / but not the way home". Of course, the psyche that led him to these imaginative underworlds could sometimes lead him back out. For instance the poem 'For My God-daughter, B.A.H'[4] joyfully concludes with the acknowledgment of the transformative power of the imagination in altering and improving reality: "for there is an Ireland, where / trees suddenly fly away / and leave their pigeons, baffled, / standing in the air".

[1] Jordan, John, Papers, National Library of Ireland, 35,041/2.
[2] Hartnett, Michael, Collected Poems, The Gallery Press, 2001.
[3] Selected and New Poems, The Gallery Press, 1994.
[4] Poems to Younger Women, The Gallery Press, 1988.

Michael Hartnett is certainly a unique Irish poet, connected and paradoxically disconnected from all the spaces in which he chose to situate himself. Seamus Heaney has said, "he's not like anybody else", a sentiment reflected in the manner he has been reconstructed in various mediums. In this anthology, which deals solely in the medium of poetry, he is variously re-imagined as a stuffed exhibited curlew, a felled willow tree, a displaced rural inhabitant, a displaced urban inhabitant, an avant-garde lyricist and a pre-Cromwellian Gaelic bard. It would thus seem that since his death Michael Hartnett has become a unique cultural symbol. A symbol that is intrinsically linked to an alternative form of Irishness; representing not so much a better Ireland but an Ireland that knows itself much more intimately. This cultural space speaks to the "identity shaken" post-Celtic Tiger Ireland very clearly. For instance, in the poem 'Willow Man' Eileen Casey remembers a reading by Michael at Virginia House in Tallaght. There is a realisation throughout her poem of what has been lost through modernisation, Virginia House has been demolished, replaced by apartment blocks and a tram line; the willow trees that lined the street felled and nothing resembles the recent past. The only consolation is that underneath the metropolis the willow's roots remain; "willow roots like language go deep", she writes. Similarly, in the poem 'The Garden Flat', Tony Curtis visits Michael's dwelling on Dartmouth Road expecting to find some solace but is alarmed at the swiftness of the transformation. The slope of the driveway had being been levelled, walls knocked, the herb garden replaced by an instant lawn, everything was brighter and "nothing was higgledy or out of place". The "filthy modern tide" of the Celtic Tiger had even swept over Michael Hartnett. Curtis concludes sombrely that "it's often much later than you think".

There are elements of grief in many of the poems written by Michael Hartnett's friends perhaps best illustrated by Theo Dorgan's 'Michael Michael' and Pauline Faye's 'The Visit'. In 'Twenty-Four Hours from Tulla' Michael Coady's grief is contrasted with the imagined celebration of Luciano Pavarotti's sixty-fifth birthday in an unusual but thought-provoking poem. While Peter Fallon's short lyric 'End' is a poem that stays with you long after you have read it. In 'An October Sun' Michael Longley pays tribute to the craftsmanship of Hartnett's poetry. Poets Valerie Sirr, Oliver Dunne and Aaron Smith lay tribute by replicating Hartnett's poetic forms, sometimes with surprising consequences. Greg O'Duill, Mike Mac Domhnaill and Caitriona Clerkin are just some of the Irish language contemporary poets featured honouring Michael.

Eavan Boland and Carol Rumens explore the mysterious elements to Michael's origins in their respective poems, while twenty year old poet Ciarán O' Rourke bestows perhaps the greatest honour on Hartnett by claiming him as a literary father in his magnificent poem 'Black Swans'.

This project has been an effort to reclaim Michael Hartnett, fifty years after he left Newcastle West and over seventy years since his birth. I wanted to gather and compile these poems in order to make sense of his legacy. The title of this bilingual anthology *I live in Michael Hartnett* is taken from Paula Meehan's inspiring poem 'Hagiography'. It aptly sums up the overall sentiments of the anthology. The literary journey that began in a meadow in Camas in West Limerick during the 1940's, when Michael's grandmother Bridget O'Halpin predicted he would become a poet continues on. Long may it continue.

James Lawlor,
Newcastle West, April, 2013

Irish Poetry
for Michael Hartnett

We always knew there was no Orpheus in Ireland.
No music stored at the doors of hell.
No god to make it.
No wild beasts to weep and lie down to it.

But I remember an evening when the sky
was underworld-dark at four.

When ice had seized every part of the city
and we sat talking —
the air making a wreath for our cups of tea.

And you began to speak of our own gods.
Our heartbroken pantheon:

No Attic light for them and no Herodotus.
But thin rain and dogfish and the stopgap
of the sharp cliffs
they spent their winters on.

And the pitch-black Atlantic night.
And how the sound
of a bird's wing in a lost language sounded.

You made the noise for me.
Made it again.
Until I could see the flight of it: suddenly

the silvery, lithe rivers of your south-west
lay down in silence.
And the savage acres no one could predict
were all at ease, soothed and quiet and

listening to you, as I was.
As if to music, as if to peace.

Eavan Boland

Gift Birds for a Poet's Christening

This one is poverty:
The home without bath and books,
Nakedness of the borrowed
Suit, the learned voice.

The fire that spreads its wings,
With earthly sighs,
Star-brewing and cave-making,
Is its argus-eyed brother.

The language carved from your side,
The lumps you'll be forced to swallow
And belch out as song
Is the blushing one.

And, still in their pale egg-shells,
Like stones in the glen,
Are the six who will collar you, pincered,
Foam-feathered, gleaming.

Carol Rumens

End
in memory of Michael Hartnett

End of sureness,
end of doubt —
when the darkness
like a light
went out.

Peter Fallon

Barn
in memory of Michael Hartnett

Hawk-attentive
between the rafters
you watched with a slow-field-gaze
as the bell-time-evening fell
so fell the bell-time-evening
falling
on the dreaming otter
falling
in and out of languages
falling
in and out of silences
falling
under the hubcap
on the gable
became a stopped clock.

Mark Whelan

Hartnett Remembered

From childhood,
West Limerick voices
Rang in his head,
In words at once familiar
But as yet unknown.
Later he followed where
Their echoes led, and found
His own Rosetta Stone
Across the severed centuries.
Poets again spoke, and
Not only in bare and barren wood,
For he brought us the music
And the song, the singer and the chord.
And when later, all too quickly,
He passed into the cold dark night
Word piles he had just found
Smouldering, because of him, will
Now burn forever, blazing bright.

Dónal O'Siodhachain

O Winged Bird

Our fathers knew each other in the music of hurling,
As we did in poems and songs, and though the years
Fill our lives with empty meeting places, I treasure
Your line 'Bóthar an fhile gan chloch mhíle air'.

There was no poetry in my milestones then, you said,
The people of Clonard and Ballymurphy would sort it out.
But I wrote my Southern Comfort in hindsight, to begin
The search for Starkie's gypsy ballads in post-Lorca Spain.

Going home to Heaney's fish-smelling balcony I found
A swallow dropped in from under the crucifying sun,
A wren handkerchiefed outside, wrapped in a blanket
From a convent bed in Santa Teresa's Encarnación.

Over dinner you let slip a jar of beetroot and for years
The stubborn stain on the tiles spoke to me of hedge birds
Claiming the ditch in spring, Templeglantine memory
Of children chasing a pig round the hillside garden.

Much of what you trawled from your travels sparkled
Afresh on the page. The day your grandmother died
During the Moroccan Madrid fling, Ó Bruadair's tortured
Tribe, the death of a Gaeltacht in Moonagay, love and exile

In the Pale, and all that *móin a' bheatha* seeping through
The veins of a dangerous little bundle, a sickly child,

Who was the worth of two poets in two languages,
Who heard 'wings of parchment shake and bells weep'.

John Liddy

Missing You
for Michael Hartnett

The goldfinch, *An Lasair Choille*[1], fires through the memory,
you and Caitlín Maude
in a wondrous combination
of strange imagery and light
out of this world.
You were always out of this world
and in an eternal hurry to be out of it too.
And yet you knew the pain of those
left in the world with no immediate way out,
no easy exit, no quick fix
in the long sentence of mourning.
No getting away from grief.

Such affection of thought
such warmth of will.
Now I follow the vacuum cleaner
along the vectors of a sunlit room,
a late autumn warming, a shaft of sun
and the dust is gathered up, filtered
and sucked into sacks
with the power of 1500 revolutions
whirring through a minute.
It frees the mind
to skimp across the shards of thought and half-thought,
the cluster of years, the voice, the playful and penetrating
brown eyes.
The long stretch of road climbing up out of Newcastle West
to curve and spill down into Teampaill Ghleantáin –
the huddle of cars at the Inn, the necklace of lights,
of houses and hamlets and hillside farms cosy
against the night, hung at points along the Glen,
and all the anger of a language fit to sell pigs in.

Rita Kelly

[1] Irish language one act play, written by M. Hartnett & C. Maude, widely produced in the 70's.

Sleeping Rough: After Rimbaud
in memory of Michael Hartnett

It's time to let myself surf on a wave that doesn't know
whether it's coming in or out. I must stop reading the
papers, and wrap them around a bottle. I could do with
a drink for the road inland to the mountain which will
shelter me.

I can walk on air when the going gets rough, and arrive
nowhere in particular, to lay my head under the stars
on a bed of green and silver as moonlight falls like sleep.
I pick up the smell of watercress once I clear my nose
in this valley of tears. Whether of joy or pain, who cares?

I hear the grass grow in the stream that runs under me.
It clouded like absinthe in my dream, and now bubbles
over with light as the day comes up. My eyes open
to a world I have almost forgotten, and I see
the mist rising on a state of mind that is at peace.

Augustus Young

The Flock

Regarding the poems. He'd say,
when I am gone, cast them
into the air like a flock of birds,
let them find their own way home.

Wind and hunters will take a few.
So too the endless stretches. The vast
ocean. Pity them on moonlit nights
when barn owl and marsh hawk quiver.

Those pale and scrawny from the start
may fall breathless from a clear blue sky,
or buckle under cloud.
no one will remember them but me:

Their downy eyes,
        their ancients songs.
All those grey feathered warblers.
All those shy, frightened creatures.

I like to imagine them migrant,
flecked against grey cloud.
Distancing themselves
with every beat of their wings.

Bless the woman who takes
them in her hands.
Bless the man who stops
to listen to their song.

Bless the woodlands
that shelter them.
Bless the child who comes
carrying a purse full of crumbs.

When their journey is over,
say ten years from now,
I know only a handful
will have made it home,

small gatherings
nesting on shelves.
Enough to make a crown of feathers,
or another necklace of wrens.

Tony Curtis

Homage to Hartnett

From Granada he brought back
Lorca's gipsy ballads.
When the blackbird whistled
in the school-hedge hedges
of Croom and Camus
he was there to listen, a naturalist,
a new and living Ó Rathaille.

In Kensington, on the underground
where nobody looks at anyone else
he looked ascetic
like a young Jean Paul Belmondo
as bony as the Rock of Skellig.

And on Leeson Street
in the Saturday crowd he was there again,
raising a glass, striking a match:
the haiku-master of Emmet Road
wedged between Sweet Afton
and Woodbine smoke.

Gerard Smyth

Ó hAirtnéide

To your poor skin and bone body,
You grappled the pain of all our past poverty,
Taking on yourself the destitution
Of scholar and sickly poet,
Making of it a song as rich
As milk in a churn gathering to gold.

While we thronged the honied avenues of prosperity,
You stood in shabby grey,
Like a forties worker waiting for a boat
(Short only of the suitcase tied with bindertwine),
Putting contradiction in our path:
And full you made us taste of the sorrow of our humanness.

We mourned ourselves in baffled Actaeon,
In Tadhg's applesweet children,
In Lorca stretched whitely on the fields of Spain:
And the agony of that Cagney woman, who left her lover's wake,
Cut into our flesh, like your death does now,
As a sliver of steel cuts the clay of the forge.

Pádraig J. Daly

Michael Hartnett, *File*

Níor chlis:
Isteach leat
Ag cuardach sa chupard dorcha
Fá dhéin na dtaibhsí sa sean-tigh
Gur gháir le háthas chugainn amach
Go raibh anois id' bhaclainn
Haicéad, Ó Rathaille, Ó Bruadair.

Amuigh faoi sholas an tráthnóna
Dúramar go rabhais ait
Ag tréigean ár gcomhluadair;
Go maith ab eol dúinn
Go raibh an áit ransáilte go minic cheana
Is cad a bheadh le fáil.

Corrdhuine a bhog go leac an tí
Thug seans dá shúile luí
Ar a raibh istigh,
Gur dhein do lorg amach;
D'éist – is tú bhí fial le caint –
Thug leis gach siolla
Feargach, cráite
Ár sinsear.

Mike Mac Domhnaill
Deireadh Fómhair 1999

The Poet Hartnett

You did not flinch:
In you went
Searching the dark cupboard
After the ghosts in the old house
Until the joyful shout came back
That you had now gathered to you:
Haicéad, Ó Rathaille and Ó Bruadair.

As we waited
In dim twilight
We thought you odd
Deserting our enjoyment;
Full well we knew
The place had been ransacked
And what was there to find…

The odd one moving to the house
Took time to focus
On the dark inside
Before they made you out;
Then listened – you had a way with words –
Brought back each syllable,
Hurt and haunted,
Of our people.

October 1999

Mike Mac Domhnaill

A Rhyme for Michael

Michael: banjo music on the Limerick train
Michael: a Jack Snipe's wing
Michael: eyes bitten like his fingernails
Michael: a smoky Poker ring

Michael: steps he stopped in the snow
Michael: 'steak-and-kidney pie'
Michael: Listen Des I have to go
Michael: the letter that never arrives

Michael: our Exchequer Street Exchange
Michael: a cheque cashed in O'Neills
Michael: a £1 note let blow away
Michael: a loan to re-connect ESB

Michael: another poet's topcoat
Michael: a broken smile
Michael: tiny handwriting in a notebook its cover biroed by a child

Desmond Egan

Copyright 1973; Desmond Egan

In-sight of you
in memory of Michael Hartnett

And just because the stand of oaks was blind
She gave them eyes; iridescent glow stones
From fathomless seas. And once inclined
To hold the sky with seasoned hands grown
Out of touch, they cupped the light, dappled
It for shadows and for shade. Now in sight
Of things they know the shape of, they grapple
With her lonely walks on moonless nights.
They whisper to each other, even the sky is alone
tonight.
She presses her eyes to their eyes and inside their world
She finds you there, naked surgeon, a light
By your well, your body unfurled
As the stars flow through you, to trace
Your hopeful song, so music is heard in space.

Eleanor Hooker

I was born in a will o the wisp
in memory of Michael Hartnett

came like a twist of the goblin past to rouse and sunder.
I am the fiend that you keep at bay, the shadow over your eye.
Try to get me out, my might is my slightness, my strength
is my veil,
the way I shroud your wish for the real
with my curling tongue on your fingers and toes, in the
whorl of your ear –
the conjure of fancy, the dropsy of drowsy, I'm there.

They think we're a light that breeds in the ghosting field
to darken the tree-held night
but we're not, we're a smolder, ash with a centre of roar,
we bide our time while you grow insurance and debt and
get older.

When they gather in halls that are named for the money
and they call for our end and muster an army
against what might happen if they upped and entered us
then we are scared –
especially of the dismantlers, they do it so well,
so fast it's the trick of conjuring nil; you don't see what is
gone.
Was there nothing there?

When one of you names us, and knows our intention
we draw you in to our inkling lair, the other dimension
and we sing together the song of no nation
that will prink and spindle the future of wish
the future of wisp at the centre of will.
I was born in a will o the wisp
and I wait here still.

Siobhan Campbell

An tIasc – The Fish

*'We breathe in our first language,
and swim in our second'.*
                    Adam Gopnik

I take my first breath from Dublin air,
snámhaim, freisin, i mBaile Átha Cliath.

English sa bhaile agus Gaeilge in school,
tá mé sáite idir na teangacha, an dá rud scaipthe.

Later, in Gaillimh, I breathe while I swim,
agus tuigim: is iasc mé, nasctha le teanga.

Tógaim mo chéad anáil i mBaile Áth Cliath,
I swim, too, in Dublin.

Béarla at home and Irish ar scoil,
I am wedged between drifting languages.

Níos déanaí, in Galway, tógaim anáil is mé ag snámh,
and I understand: I am a fish, hooked on language.

Nuala Ní Chonchúir

So What If There's No Happy Ending?
in memoriam Michael Hartnett

So what if there's no happy ending?
Don't be afraid of the dark;
Open the door into darkness
And hear the black dogs bark.

Oh what a wonder is darkness!
In it you can view
The moon and stars of your nature
That daylight hid from you.

Open the door into darkness,
There's nothing at all to fear —
Just the black dogs barking, barking
As the moon and stars appear.

Gabriel Fitzmaurice

Adharca Broic
in ómós do Mhícheál Ó hÁirtnéide

Níor shamhlaíos adharca riamh leis an mbroc
An créatúr cúlánta ag tochailt leis sa dorchadas
Ag éalú ón duine, ag teitheadh lena anam,
Ach thug tú ábhar machnaimh dom:

Níor scorn leat siúl sna bratóga le hEoghan
An Bhéil Bhinn ná le Dáibhí Ó Bruadair féin
A mhéara marbh ón bhfeac, a dhínit slán fós,
Ag díriú a rachta ar ghramaisc a chráite.

Sheas tú leo nuair a d'fhág tú slán leis an mBéarla,
Ainneoin féith na filíochta, tú imithe le fuacht is le fán,
Deighilte amach ó do mhuintir i muinín an bhraoin,
Bús deataigh ag dalladh do shúl is dod thachtadh tirim.

Feicim fós tú, ag rianadh easnacha an duine
Mar chlaiseacha prátaí le linn an Drochshaoil
Gan teacht riamh ar theanga d'ealaíne, id fháidh
Ar do thairseach féin ag cur adharca fileata uair, ar bhroc.

Declan Collinge

Note: Ó Teachtaireacht Téacsa Coiscéim 2007

Between

Fresh breeze that swept the Irish Sea,
flung spray up on the rocky tongue
on which we sat in trembling wind
as one tongue slipped from this to that,
a fish flip-flopping on its back.

Sometimes it stalls – unsure, uncertain –
and becomes distressed before
flash-forwarding to the next.

Tongues flit between two foreign spots,
they curve and curl and jut out of
my mouth. Two tongues working as one,
they fight – protest – against those words:
still guttural yet lyrical.

Louise Hegarty

Féinphortráid ag Brionglóideach

"Ag cuimhneamh as Béarla, ag taibhreamh as Gaeilge"
                                        Michael Hartnett.

Trí mo néalta milse
Titeann braonta báistí
Na filíochta
Gabhaim buíochas sa chiúnas,
Amhail leamhan a lúbann
I dtreo lasair.

                    Doiréann Ní Ghríofa

Prioba-nan-Sùl

Chì mi reult-na-maidine
Tro fhàrlas m' òige
'S bidh mi a' dùnadh mo shùl
'S a' bruadar fad caogad bliadhna
'S a' toirt air ais a h-uile h-àrd is ìseal.
Bidh mi a' fosgladh mo shùl agus an sin
Tha reult-na-h-oidhche 's gun fhiosta
Tha camhanaich an fheasgair ann.

Rody Gorman

Note: Translation of Michael Hartnett's *'Blink of an Eye'* into Scottish Gaelic

For Michael Hartnett

You wore an outsized cap
Of the kind
One might find
In a stall in Rathkeale
On a fair day;
Yet still, it sat snugly enough
On your unkempt crown;
With your ploughman's gait
I watched you, more than once,
Negotiate the banks
Of the Grand Canal,
On the arm, betimes,
Of the lady
(Your partner);
She had, it seemed,
A certain aura
Of long-suffering;
At the end, I suppose,
It was the brandy
That bore you up.
The first poem by you
That ever I read
Was in a slim collection
Through which I browsed
In the Eblana bookshop
On Grafton Street
In 1969.
(Its owners, decent folk,
Were endlessly indulgent;
Generous was the space
That they afforded;
We browsed, but rarely bought),.

Your baby sister's eyes,
Sealed in death,
Had once, you said,
Been thrush's eggs;
Repeatedly,
Your father
Interjected:
'How goes the night, Boy'?
At the end of all you told him:
'It is dawn'!
I recall still
The catch in my throat
From that dialogue drawn.

The first time
Ever I talked to you
Was in the National Library;
You had papers for sale,
Which,
With no haggling on either side,
We bought.

One day – not long, I'd say
Before you passed away –
I called on you.
You were setting out places
For dinner guests;
'Did you know', you said,
'I trained as a chef?
Desserts, boy,
Were my *specialité*!'

Already you'd set up
Elaborate confections,
Sculpted to a turn;
But I had come
To look
At a residue
Of your literary stuff;
With a fine irreverence
You termed it
'The scrapings of my old barrel'!
You took me through
To show it
In the kitchen;
It proved
Interesting enough.

We emerged to discover
A large and portly tom
Perched easily upon
Your table, demolishing
One of your delicate
Confections;
'Bold pussy!' *Bold* pussy!'
You intoned,
Cuffing him gently
Round his well-upholstered gob,
Until he chose,
Eventually,
To take himself off.

Unphased,
In the refrigerator
You deposited all,
Securely;
Save only target
Of that errant Tom,
Which you proceeded,
There and then,
To replenish, resculpt, repair;
That too, when you had done,
You made to put away,
But stopped abruptly,
Pirouetted on one foot,
Then poised,
Nuyerev-like,
With contrite mien,
You proffered it:
'Gerry', you said,
'Didn't I clean forget?
Shur, maybe ... ...
You might like a bit'?

Gerry Lyne

The Princess of Sorrows
in memory of Michael Hartnett

The Princess of Sorrows blames herself
and cannot disguise it. For too long now
she has sat on this footpath and no longer knows
the way home. In the hostel she feels
she will one day be invisible, even to herself.
On nights like this only a doorway
seems solid. So five nights a week
she comes to sit here, her head to one side,
as though the fall or the blow
that has scarred her nose since yesterday
had snapped her neck. Rag-doll princess,
inner child of the inner city
set adrift, I touch your sleeve,
I drop a note in your paper cup;
I greet you in English, in Irish, in Greek,
or something that sounds like Greek; I speak
Lorca's Spanish, the Latin of Catullus,
two or three words of Romanian learned
one night in a bar from two drunken thieves
equally lost ... And then it ends, passes,
the dance that's inside me, and I tip
the tip of my cap, clicking my heels
like poetry's Fred Astaire, and bow
low before you in inherited shame
at having so little to offer you here
on this Baggot Street night, in this Baggot Street rain,
where the cars flow past in a river of lights,
and we are not strangers, not any more,
but the Princess of Sorrows and Hartnett the poet,
each of us homeless in every language known.

Pat Boran

Templeglantine

A village that is nothing
But a few farmhouses.
Not a soul outside.
Wind and rain are hunting
This hill-sheltered town land.

Roads like lashes
On a bare back.
Indented, fringed
By hedges, boosted
Like earth along a furrow.

Beyond a curve, finally,
His white remembered house
In altered light.
The view from there bumps
Abruptly against a hill.

Maybe he was looking,
Like I was, for what's forever lost.
But there is no return
That is not blurred
Or erased by alcohol.

Huib Fens

In a Corner of O'Neills
for Michael Hartnett

In O'Neills of Suffolk Street
(but Church Lane too,
or Lana Cille, if you wish)
he turned to me and said
'I'm leaving English, Brendan.
I'm going back to Irish.'

'Why?' I asked.

'I have to' he replied. 'I simply have to.'
And then,
'What do you think?'

Silence a while.

'You're saying goodbye to English.
That's like leaving someone near and dear.
Have you found a nearer, dearer love?
Maybe you should say why
You're choosing to say good-bye?'

'Is it a choice' he murmured,
'or a compulsion?'
'That's for you to say.
Either way
you're saying good-bye.
Say why.'

'I will' he said.
'I'll say farewell to English.
Beannacht Dé ort. Slán leat.'

In a corner of O'Neills
we drank to that.

Brendan Kennelly

Hartstown Haiku
after 'Inchicore Haiku' by Michael Hartnett

Ice-cream van jingles
echo across the estates —
kids knock back vodka

Unexpected flash
of a Maynooth bound night train —
vagrant is noticed

Estate agent sign
staked in a terraced garden —
three more down the road

Valerie Sirr

M.H

I

Hat pulled down, he whispers
A poem in your ear —
Is it a greeting or farewell?

II

Blackbird —
With yellow nib
And ink.

Oliver Dunne

Epilogue
for Michael Hartnett

Like a wren he was,
bright and quick and brown,
head angled to miss no trick.
Hair like down

brushed, feathered
around the black bird
eyes. And what
a sound we heard

from that almost-elusive
wren-poet,
half-hidden,
giving full throat

to all he saw or felt
we missed. For any
naturalist of song
to hear. And he

flits among the brambles
of our thoughts. His song
caught, hedged 'round,
a sound that proves them wrong.

Paul Ó Colmáin

From Golden Hell, A Dream

'I put the plug in.
Mozart comes into the room
riding a cello.'

My liver looks up
from the bottom of a glass,
snug in golden hell.'

> *— Inchicore Haiku - 1985*
> M. Hartnett

Hartnett reading aloud
some of his haiku
and
> Mozart coming into the room
> riding a chip

is it mine?
half a dozen in the audience
fumbling for their mobiles

and then Michael waltzing
out of sight.

>   *Liam O'Meara*

Saint Michael's Estate

Hartnett knew the subtlety of it
when he lived in Inchicore
'watching the slums
replace his tribal village
and old barracker'

Subverters in pinstripe
demolished Keogh Square
brick by brick
held together
by archetypal memory

when it was Richmond Barracks
the men of the Rising taken there
after a night spent in the open
the leaders shot
the rank and file transported

The land re-zoners
and gerrymanderers
learned their trade well
divide and conquer
carve up the community
isolate the dissenters
and stack them up
in concrete boxes.

Teri Murray

That Night in Tallaght

There was that night in Tallaght
when close together we spoke *as Gaeilge*.
And, being within The Pale, it seemed strange
to others present there,
when we discussed our love
of Federico Garcia Lorca
and other things Spanish, in Irish.

Your hand shook violently
and red Spanish wine splashed
onto your cleanest dirty shirt.
Your eyes caught mine
and an Inchicore Haiku ensued
dripping from your loosened lips.

I could not halt hot tears from dripping
down my cheeks onto my poetry-event finery
whilst you reached for another
plastic glass of Spanish wine and shouted
My Dark Rosaleen, Remember Limerick!

Mae Leonard

Willow Man

*After a visit by Michael Hartnett to Virginia House, Tallaght,
July 1993*

He arrived late in a pre-booked taxi but I would have waited
even longer for that first glimpse of him leaning
through the doorway as if a birthing were taking place,
shoulders coming first,
this small, dark man with brooding eyes,
tweed jacket, cap peaked as a diviner's rod.

Half in, half out, he seemed unsettled
like a foal first finding its awkward stride
before shufflings of paper, his voice growing strong,

clear well water, child-like magic

spilling from his mouth.

Poems drifted outside where willow branches
wound their paths as voices did he connected up
from the Telephone Exchange in Exchequer Street.
It must have pleased him, those conversations
flying on witcheries of wire through air.

That tree, symbol for wisdom, *Salix*
(he knew its Latin name)
is long gone. Disappeared too, Virginia House.
Replaced by shape shifting landscape,
apartment blocks rising like totem poles.
A Luas Line snakes its way to a city of many tongues.

We are different yet the same since he was here.

Dublin Mountains tower still behind our houses,
thrushes sing with wrens in Gleann na Smól,
winds sweep away winter's ghosts,
moon and stars sickle our skies,

willow roots, like language, go deep.

Eileen Casey

Curlew Sandpiper in the Natural History Museum
for Michael Hartnett

Always a startle
to see it
still there,

pinned
to a split
second,

head bent,
at work
and wary,

one eye
sharp
for departure,

delicately,
quick-wittedly
winged,

thin beak
all instinct

  Mark Roper

Letter to Michael, August 2008

Dear Mister Hartnett,
   I have long been an admirer of your work
'Tis sorry I am our paths never crossed.
I went to school with a young brother of yours
Raneen we called him, the small wren.
Met another brother once,
He said he did not think much
Of wasting time reading poetry in pubs
He'd rather cards or horses.
   Don't know where to post this,
Upper or Lower Maiden Street.
Sure Newcastle West will find you
They know your name.
   North Quay was flooded last week
And down by your old Scoil,
Cars were washed down the Arra
By School House Lane
Timber floated in furniture showrooms
Wine bottles bobbled in eating houses.
What a waste that was Michael.
Rich and poor, shopkeepers and paupers
They were all hit.
But still, through it all
People were great to their neighbours.
   The flood was at one in the morning
When the current went off
People were in pure darkness
The old people were terrified.
No one died.
Weren't the old people clever long ago
When they left Maiden Street

For the higher ground of the Park.
   I must go now, Michael, mind yourself.

Signed,
   A poet

PS I will send you on my latest work soon.
The Peaceful River Arra.
Joe Healy

Twenty-Four Hours from Tulla

Stopping for a leak in the County Limerick
suddenly I slip into the deep of the world,
after midnight and the stars upstanding,
engine idling and radio on, with Pavarotti
sending *E lucevan le stelle*[1] up
into the night and out across
blind fields where distantly
a beast is bellowing some distress.

I too am in the dark
as I piss into a ditch
to an aria from Tosca,
just over the threshold
of the thirteenth of October
in the year two thousand –
Pavarotti's birthday, the presenter said,

and also, as it happens, a poet's
anniversary: a year to the day
since, peeling potatoes at the sink,
I was ambushed by the news
of Michael Hartnett's passing,
itemised before the latest
update on the weather.

But bravo, Luciano, bravo!
Wherever you are I'm sure
candles are alight, corks
popping, music swelling for
your sixty-fifth live lap around the sun.

[1] The Stars Were Shining.

Meanwhile, back in Newcastle West,
my greetings to you, Michael,
after your first solar circuit
under sod in Calvary Cemetery
where all are teetotallers
and no one complains.

I don't miss chats we never had
about poetics or postmodernism
whenever our paths crossed, but that
running ad lib game we made
of relocating songs —

I want to be a part of it —
New Ross, New Ross!
you might insist,

while I'd respond with Kilfenora,
where the wind comes sweeping down the plains
and one could meet a *spéir-bhean*

tall and tan and young and lovely,
the Girl from Inchigeelagh,
lost and lonely in the Burren.

Be sure of this, you'd say,
if I was there she'd sidle up
beside me at the bar

and sing into my ear —
Fly me to Macroom
and let me play among the stars.

How little I know, Michael,
in this here and now, and what
I think I understand reduces day by day
as though I gravitate towards
a baseline of unknowing
that may (for all I know)
be bliss.

E lucevan le stelle.
In what townland am I standing?
Tell me the name of that star up there –
no, not the bright one
but the fainter one behind it
(*behind* it?).

Anyway, what's in a name,
and who do I think I'm asking?
Dark or day it's always
someone's birthday
or the birthday of their death.
So all together now –
Michael, myself, Sinatra,
Puccini, Luciano –

Fill my heart with song
and let me sing forevermore.

Michael Coady

The Garden Flat

I called to where Michael used to live on Dartmouth Road.
Though I knew his shadow would be gone from the window,
I thought I'd find his coffee cup, his book open on the table.
But everything was gone. A life cleared up and packed away.
Walls were knocked down. Things papered and painted.
Everything was brighter. There was a big glass window
and a Chinese vase where the garage doors use to be.
Out in the garden, someone had dug up the herbs he's planted.
Things were raked over, ready for the arrival of the instant lawn.
Nothing was higgledy or out of place. They had even levelled
The slope in the drive. You couldn't roll home anymore, just couldn't.
But the dizzy miracle was, the morning I called there'd been
a light fall of snow and a set of footprints lead away from the door.
I just missed him. It's often much later than you think.

Tony Curtis

Death of an Ulsterwoman

Unbending, in the sense
that she was arthritic
in both hands and hips,
and upright, in the sense
that she kept secrets in the eye
between blasts of truth telling —
leaving her free to work
while others slept.
Yet resigned, in the end
to a projection of life
on the television screen;
steeping slowly for silent hours
in memories incessant
as the drizzling rain.
I loved her from the day she died.

She was a sermon to an empty church.
She was an impromptu bunch of chrysthanthemums.
She was an end to an unfair fight.
She was a glass of sherry to the New Year.
She was a mother burying an only child.
She was an old bible, full of voided words.

Aaron Smith

Death of an Irishman
for Michael Hartnett

Ignorant of nothing. Proud, fierce, pagan,
wearing a necklace of wrens, long-dead now,
and making songs for all Ireland to sing
in Irish. No meagre voice, even in
the twisted tongue so fit for selling pigs.
Poet head shows a kiss for father, knows
the small white burial of a three years child.
How goes the night without you, man? Gone, now,
the small wristlets of rain, the summer dance
at the crossroads. We came a long way then,
your thin child's purse full of galaxies.

Cathy Bryant

In Memoriam Michael Hartnett

When we drank
He sometimes asked for a cartoon for his partner
If he was late
Or one over the eight.

Months after he died,
Opening her bag she asked, 'Remember these?'
Bar doodles: fish, rhinoceri, a dog with wings.
A child's purse full of useless things.

Tom Matthews

Móin na nGé[1]

The signpost in Irish made sense
my mother's pronunciation,
all those years of Monagea,
in my mind's eye, one evening
at Camas just saying good-bye,
a gaggle of slow geese

bustling across the road-field
to the pond by the gate
in a straggling line, imperious,
serene, ladies in white flounced lace
in late summer heat ambling to a ball,
ready at the least inspection

to take umbrage, lift wings
and flap, rush long snake-like necks
across the stand at us and hiss,
flightless birds, poised for
ambush or take off,
 gleaned in advance –

nothing to do with a golden egg,
more: precious goose fat,
strongest quills pared for a pen,
downy feathers plucked
for a quilt, beside the range,
that sinewy span, a goose-wing.

Catherine Phil MacCarthy

[1] Goose Marsh

Black Swans
for Michael Hartnett

To plant in the bitter wind
a pure note, to make of the gravel-stone
an oat-seed, golden in the loam.

In dim meadows you clicked
your tongue, and the black swans
of dialect came with their webbed feet
and ancient wings, dappling
the waters.

You tapered too, thirsting,
between river-bank and the deep,
terrible currents, and the birch tree
murmured from the sap against
your steadied palm.

Now we also strain to walk
the old ways, amid reeds and rugged
pools where once your shadow
wavered; to find

in the hardened earth
a dark space, from which
a white flower
may grow.

Ciarán O'Rourke

The Elementalist

This is what you reach for
As you reach for your glass - the almost uncontained
Leap of the wave, the furnace
Of breath as the white flock flies,
And its horn-notes, riper than speech,
And its collective dream:

This. Not the shadow-patrol
With wings at half-mast, faithful
To the cold river's centrifuge,
And the five descending swamps —
Hand-span of our bodily journey
But not the whole journey.

Sometimes it flies, and the blackness
Is nothing but the smoke
Of a long dusk; it folds into the sunset
And you reach again and again for the black swan's
flight
Spinning mad in a room spun mad
At the farthest corner of the city.

But it comes no closer on the mountain
Than in the hollow glass,
No finer in the tiny rock-rose
Than the un-fairy-rings of yesterday's slopped solvent.
Whatever you can retrieve
And keep written, poet, will be reached for,

And leap with the next wave's leaping
And breathe with the white flock, flying.

Carol Rumens

Closing the Ears
in memory of Michael Hartnettt : 1941-1999

Closing the ears of the dead
Was harder when eyes were blind
To all but funeral's affectation.

A fly parades its vanity on the faces' vein.

Tightening the hands together
In an unsaid prayer. Embracing
Music's colour. A hill of knuckles

Turning white. The harmony of blasphemy.

A street flood pausing to climb
Over nameless faces. Proceeding.
Following. Instincts killing.

Guilt is patterned. Distanced.
Seamed with taut threads pulling
Ever towards the distance of difference.

Hayden Murphy

Michael and the Angel

Stop, said the angel.
Stop doing what you were doing and listen.
Yes, you can taste the stew and add the salt.
(Have you tried it with a touch of cinnamon?)
But listen to me while you're doing it.
I am not the one who found you
The work in the Telephone Exchange.
That was a different angel.
I am the angel who says remember,
Do you remember, the taste of the wood-sorrel leaves
In the ditches on your way to the school? Go on,
Remember, how you found them
Piercing a lattice of green blades,
And their bitter juice. The grassy roads
That swung in and out of the shade
Passing a well or a graveyard,
The gaps and stiles on the chapel path –
Their windings, their changes of pace
Always escaping the casual watch you kept –
You must go back and look at them again,
And look again the next day, for they change,
There is new growth, or the dew is packed like a blanket;
Later come rose hips and the bloom of sloes,
And you must be there to see them. Your children will find
The sweet drop in the fuchsia flower, swallow it down,
They will run from the summer shower, but your work is to stay,
To hold the pose of the starved pikemen, holding upright
The borrowed long ladder. After the rain
dries off your shrinking shirt, the blue flower
Will shine up from the aftergrass where it nestled.

You must search for the words for the steam rising off the field —
You might find them there, among the scattered grain.

Eiléan Ní Chuilleanáin

Resurrection
A Tribute to Michael Hartnett

Twenty thousand doors
abruptly slammed in my face
— cast out of my place.

Being damned with faint praise
— the blight of my twilight days
Death sees me reborn

To sup with the poor
a ghostly diminutive form
My joy rekindled.

Michael O'Flanagan

Flesh and Bone
in fond memory of Michael Hartnett

You're safer dead
They can praise you and avoid your eye

More praised by far
Now that your quiet roar is silent

More lauded now
That there's no risk of a blow from your tongue

More written about
Now that you can't add your own commentary

More welcome
Now that you'll never arrive

The poet should be a gentleman
But seldom a man
Being both you were twice shunned

Twice damned and double-tongued
While gold was thrown
At the split-tongued and the soul-dead

Made out of words is flesh and bone
Enough
Made out of verse is better –

Better to be drunk and singing
Than sober and sullen
Better to be a poet than a kicked pup

You're safer dead
Than to have to hear
Praise from the pen dipped in the purse

No one like you now
Nor then
No one like you to scald us again.

Fred Johnston

In Memory of M.H and Grandma

He now no longer wished to live, but die,
and catch, by any means at all,
the peoples' and God's eye
(as poets, when no longer breathed on,
by the muses breath).
In Tunisia he was stoned to death.
          from; *"He'll To The Moors"* by Michael Hartnett

In love with virgin Christ
Our grandmas then in black and beads
Their spouses dead, were nuns possessed
Praying the truth of Eternal Wisdom.

Speech hummed in toothless anecdote
They parable'd us in moral rectitude,
Pagan invective. Believing God
Enjoyed himself - laughed heartily,
Knowing Satan burned in Hell for all
Eternity, as with all disloyal devils.

Through a kneading mix of love and fear,
They clouded us in starched humanity.
Made ghosts real; visible in our heads.
Did not see reason to search for God
As He was in evidence everywhere.
Veritas and joy reigned mocking over
Sin, from vast planned space and time.

Made us passionate about losses, things
We might not have found in a hundred lifetimes.
Inspired us to drop ignorance for the intellectual.
Stay true to magic, and the elegance of poetry.
We dug our own graves, drank our own poison.

Donal O'Flynn

Four Meta-Haiku
in memory of Michael Hartnett

Money suits black robes
.   jackals barking with light shadows
Burren flowers remain

For Irish Artists

Some wish to corral
one or the other or both
love runs free with each

Horse & Child

Picture motion glass
convalescent home stale air
saved by dancing dreams.

Not Home

River water here
standing quite still   waiting for
yourself to appear.

Actualization

B. D. MacMahon

Incommunicado
with apologies to Michael Hartnett

Disappointment, uninvited, steps
in between us; stretching
its metal, silver screen
where words and thoughts
like summer midges, or night-
time moths of black and red,
beat and batter their wings,
      exhaust themselves;
never making it through
from one side to
the other.

Eibhlín Nic Eochaidh

Seedling
in memory of Michael Hartnett

Asleep in the loft of his granny's house
He heard her speak Gaelic to her crony friends

Awake in the lap of God, he listened, unaware
All the while being prepared to savour

The word, so perfectly in his child's mind
As to make it an oyster of fine pearls.

Marian Finan Hewitt

Final Version
in memory of Michael Hartnett

Too early. Yes, all of that. But now you've said
A farewell to all language, and are translated
To a version where, definitively yourself,
Sharing elements with hares and otters,
And raising pewter mugs with spailpín poets,
You can hear the pulse-music you knew well
Lies beyond all poems, and before them,
And cannot be lost in the translation.

Paddy Bushe

Life
in memory of Michael Hartnett

The taste of drink: the subtle off-tang of white wine,
the bitter slug of stout, the burning nip of brandy,
the sourness of beer, swigged, quaffed and sipped; life
distilled or fermented, distastefully
hitting the spot with a taste of more, an aftertaste
bequeathing a haunting sense of the perfect.

Greg Delanty

"The Act of Poetry is a Rebel Act"
Michael Hartnett

Possibly those inquisitive eyes
Grasped the horizon
Of his wonder gift,
Telltales of lift-the-heart
Follies - like addressing the statue
In Killtimagh of a brandy-shadowed
Morning: No wars of mercy fought
On his behalf. His waging, lonesome
As any poet's playing the poker
Of "see you, raise you" till its echo tumbled
From the kitty of common sense
How well he knew
"the act of poetry
is a rebel act."

Leland Bardwell

After Reading Michael Hartnett

All of the temporary settlements we come to
have the loving feel of permanence
but too much
the smell of cinnamon and coriander, honey,
pinned and mounted butterflies,
unwearable golden shoes;
when this act, of all acts,
is supposed to be a rebel act.
Break camp.
In the morning we have to move on anyway.
Overnight the weather has changed.

Joe Horgan

Eoghan Rua on His Deathbed
for Mícheál Ó hAirtnéide

Sad indeed is the poet when his pen
slips quietly from his grip before he dies,
in a hut far from towns and the laughter
of men whose tongues are dense with inherited
words. And sad are the poems which throng in his head
like children locked in a classroom.
No, porter cools his mouth that once –
'some handsome woman christianed sweet, no
sunlight strikes his hut that even the winds ignore.
Sad indeed is the poet when his pen
slips quietly from his grip before he dies.

Seán Dunne

A Farewell to Hartnett

Quiet mutterer of profundities
Laced with such understated humour
As my rural relatives visited on me
Years ago if I tried my townie ways,
You have slipped out the back door
During a lull in the conversation
When someone turned up the RTE news.

We expected you back any minute
Your face creased with lasting laughter
And some story bubbling on your lips
That would have eager elbows leaning
From afar, 'what was that?' as the gales arose.
But you didn't return having set off

To share a good one with the gossiping stars.

Christopher Murray

The Visit
Éigse Michael Hartnett, September 2003

As visitors do
I thought to bring
armfuls of flowers
or a single stem
graceful with dew,
searched each shop display
for the perfect petalled gift,
thought of culling wild woodbine
from hedgerows
or the bright red berries
winter birds feed on,
but arrived with empty hands
took, instead of gave,
a pebble from your grave.

Pauline Fayne

Níl sa saol ach...

Puth ghaoithe,
buillín sa tsruth
cleite ag cleitearnach
barr ribe, fás ingne,
puth anála, cuisle chroí
greim láimhe, rith fola
téad snátha
briseadh uibhe
pléascadh síl
bachlóg ag oscailt
duilleog ar chraobh
fás aon lae
carsán seanduine
gáire linbh

Éalú idir cleith is ursain
idir mian agus éigean
idir gáire agus gol
idir grá agus fuath
idir codladh agus múscailt

Éalaíonn muid
ón chaonach liath
is ón fhothruicear leathchochta i gcónaí

Níl sa saol ach...
clic cleaic
giob geab
sifil seaifil

Haemaitít leathmharbh díbheo
Leath is
murlach mara
nó an t-iasc ag peilteáil sa líon
an leanbh ag léim sa bhroinn

Sin an saol
nach ait an iníon í
a imíonn chomh gasta le casacht chrua thirim
Cas arís orainn, a Thiarna, impímid
Bí ag guí ar ár sonsa
muidinne áta gafa i gcíor thuathail
gafa in uige an dáin
muidinne nach dtig linn guí
Bronn orainn síocháin.

Caitríona Ní Chléirchín

Éigse Michael Hartnett 2002

I will be there in spite of death
for ink speaks and paper speaks
  Michael Hartnett – alias The Wasp

> *…whom can you touch, or love,*
> *in two half-languages?*
>   Vincent Buckley

Among white sepulchres,
the overpowering eight-feet-high angels' wings,
a glitter of gold letters on polished marble
and plastic flowers garish under artificial red candles
eternally flickering their battered watch
in Newcastle West graveyard,

you lie simply
beneath the grey stone
– no frippery for the Wasp –
wreathed in your necklace of wrens
hovering effortless round one word:
        File.

So small they are, those birds,
to be killed instead of kings,
to be full of secrets,
leaving the scar of their gift on you,
the living flame of your spliced tongue –
two languages to engrave the page.

                    Robyn Rowland

Note: This is an extract from a longer poem by Robyn Rowland

Listen

You throw the stale broken bread
out the back door of your grandmother's house
you hide then, watching out through the window
on the roof and tree they wait –

looking, listing, searching,
afraid it could be a trap –
so they wait
as you watch –
silently

deep in your own over active mind
as the first sentence of a poem
flies straight out –
the long journey now begins
starting with
isolation –
Long hours locked trapped
deep in your own mind
oblivious of the world around you
searching for the final word.

Leonard Holman

Samhailteacha de Mhícheál

Oibrí malartáin idirnáisiúnta,
leabhar filíochta ar a ghlúin, ag breacadh lae,
cóipleabhar oscailte os a chomhair, peann réidh.

Teach beag i gceantar oibrithe iarnróid
Inse Chór, ráillí iarainn loighic an fhile
ag lúbadh faoi ghrian ionsparáide

Duine beag mór, file nach sásta
iall a chur ar chois bainbh
is a thabhairt chun a reicthe ar aonach.

Ní torc a cuireadh faoina mhuineál
ach muince dreoilín, forba faoina n-ingne
nach leigheasann lia nocht.

Gabha geal oilte aistritheora,
leannán seanmhná faoi fhallaing veilvit aige sin
ba chapall ráis faoi thrucail, dallóga air.

A dhuine dhorcha shorcha, mo bhruadair,
mo ghiolla mear, mo phádraigín na croise, éistim do ghreann,
tostaim roimh do shotal, amharcaim d'fhoighne chrainn:
do dhroim le búir, le móir is álainn ainneoin ualaigh.

Chimil tú scian leis an chloch fhaobhair, suas, anuas,
faobhar an chruach ina lann in aghaidh easa
a raibh docharchú gonta ar a chúl, bradán éigse
faoina chrúib, faoina fhiacail.

Thiar ort sa deireadh, tú thoir, thugadar an
tseanmhallacht ghloine
duit, an scáthán cam, nó lúth do theanga is a grástúlacht
níor thuig said,
ná cnó a brí, ach lean tú, lean, is scaoil amach na páistí
gréine ba thoradh ar an suirí ghrá
ealaíne, iad ag imeacht glórach geal gáireata ar
shráideanna cathrach.

Gréagóir Ó Dúill

West Going West

Walking down O'Curry Street
and looking at Egan's Marble Bar...is this where it
was...Kilkee
where we danced in the sea
in winter...
myself Gail Price and Michael Hartnett
before being run out of town
by the Sergeant
more than their several lives ago
and to think like exclusion
we might have made it important:

The man I hire the bike from
could he have heard the story?
Or the present staff
of the Bank Of Ireland
where they cashed me a cheque for a fiver
drawn on trust
identity being the poem I recited
while word by word they followed the text

More than forty years ago:
and my benefactor John McCarter
has long since joined the martyrs
in Letterkenny of the traffic lights
prophesied by Columcille:

And I cannot get back to today
the starting-point of itself
till I stop
for bread and milk in Carrigahoult:

You're a writer then –
you write yourself?
I'm quizzed by the man in the shop
Do you know James Liddy?
Or Brendan Kennelly?

On my long trip West
on this stony road
I keep my counsel still
on falling foul of the beatitudes –
and...the loneliness...
of their rejection –
for dancing in the sea one winter here
before
being run out of town by the Guards:

surviving
the same crooked passing of time
and the strange imperfect Masonry of poets.

Macdara Woods

Oidhreacht Mhichíl

Nár mhair Eoghan Rua
Idir do dhá shlinneán
Ag fuascailt aislingí
As a shí-chruit
Go dtí go bhfuair tú an chaint?

Nár thug sé leis thú
Ag crú na mba
Ar Bhealach na Bó Finne
Mar, as coire na réaltaí,
Nár steall tú, thál tú
Dúch do dhúchais
Anuas ar bhallaí Luimnigh!

Ní tirimede ár súil tuile do véarsaí:
Dubhach sinn i d'éagmais
Faoi néal chomh liath le broc,
Ag feitheamh le bogha ceatha
Ar mhullach na cathrach,
Claíomh solais mar a bheadh conradh,
Ach is leabhar thú anois i mo láimh,
Dornán dánta a sheachnaíonn sinn ar ár n-aimhleas.

Derry O'Sullivan

An October Sun
in memory of Michael Hartnett

Something inconsolable in you looks me in the eye,
An October sun flashing off the rainy camber.
And something ironical too, as though we could
warm our hands at turf stacks along the road.

Good poems are as comfortlessly constructed,
each sod handled how many times. Michael, your
poems endure the downpour like the skylark's
chilly hallelujah, the robin's autumn song.

Michael Longley

Note: From *Snow Water*, Cape Poetry, 2004

Nine Mays Later
in memory of Michael Hartnett

Michael:
   It is not my green garden
   on this misty May morning
   that makes me sad all that
   transfer of emotion
   to the external seen
   landscape is so yesterday,
   all that Wordsworthian
   personification
   no, this melancholy
   is purely personal,
   completely internal.

Yesterday a book arrived
with tributes and memories
compiled by your son, Niall
*Notes From His Contemporaries:
A Tribute to Michael Hartnett*
reading it caused my sadness,
remembering distant days
in Leeson Street and the Green,
you declaiming your sweet verse
in that lilting voice of yours.

This May morning a fine mist
envelops my garden
so green, lush & full of life:
but the light is dull, sky grey,
as silence pervades this room
where I sit and remember.

Enough gloom: we need music
and a sean-nós singer,
a Limerick fiddler
and a pure tin-whistler
taking flight like a songbird,
dispelling all melancholy.

May, 2009

Hugh McFadden

Michael Michael

Michael, I was on the East Link in a taxi when the nurse
In my ear said, soft and sad, I'm afraid your friend is dead.

A wind out of Munster shook the bridge.

We stopped and I stepped to the parapet. October flowed
In the black Liffey below. Ebb tide, by the slanting buoys.

A wind out of Munster shook the bridge.

I closed my eyes, went down and in for Ó Rathaille, Ó Bruadair,
That stiff-eyed company of the living still —

A wind out of Munster shook the bridge.

A wren darted from hedge to hedge and then followed it
With their eyes, their hand lifted in welcome —

A wind out of Munster shook the bridge.

The wren became a wraith became a stately air, turned
Through the bony hands of a watchful piper.

A wind out of Munster shook the bridge.

What shall we do for timber? The last of the woods are down
And our quiet master down. I got back in, we drove to the toll.

A wind out of Munster shook the bridge.

The driver paid and asked was I all right, would we go on?
Drive on, I said, drive on. He was a good man.

And the wind behind us shook the bridge.

Theo Dorgan

Michael Hartnett, The Poet King

The poet went to his hotel room and sitting on the edge of
the bed wished he were dead.
"O God," he said, "I have had enough. Take my life; I am no
better than my ancestors."
Then he lay down and went to sleep.
But his soul stayed awake and said, "Get up and eat."
He rummaged in his carrier bag and found a doughnut and
a bottle of still water.
He ate and drank and then lay down again.
But his soul said to him a second time, "Get up and eat, or
you will not be able to give the poetry reading tonight."
So he got up and ate and drank, and made a cup of tea with
a teabag, and strengthened by that food he went on giving
poetry readings for forty years until he reached the hospital
where he gladly, not sadly, died.
Forty years ago he would have been glad to know that forty
years later he would gladly, not sadly, die.

Paul Durcan

Note: From *The Art of Life,* The Harvill Press, 2004.

Remembering Michael

The Force and fire of the incoming wave
Subsume the wave withdrawing.
The fruitfulness of the fruit
Is part of the flower's dying.
The fruit falls to the loamy earth
To begin a new tree's growing;
And the sea devours its waves
Less bliss should end its flowing.

Anthony Cronin

Adhlacadh an Dreoilín[1]
in memory of Michael Hartnett
Calvary cemetery, Newcastle West, 16 October 1999

You were a wren in your ways and shapes,
king of the birds that could roost in the holly,
land on a leaf or dart to the light,
drop out betimes and go into hiding –

just as now in your tidy nest
you're home and dry though the heavens open
to spill down on our heads and hearts
the clouds' overflow out in Calvary cemetery.

Far from us now the day in John B's
we attempted to rise to *An Clár Bog Déil*[2]
on the coat-tails of The Limerick Rake,
and Bacchus sporting with Venus.

I can foretell the past, you said,
and once, when quizzed by a student at Queen's
about where you stood on religion:
I'm a catalyst. But I'm a Roman catalyst.

Little you weigh as they let you down
and you with Ó Bruadair under your belt
along with Haicéad and Ó Rathaille
and all your own hatchings in our two tongues.

When you're tucked away we traipse back to town,
chastened stragglers of the standing army
with west Limerick mud on our soles and uppers,
agus fágaimid siúd mar atá sé.[3]

Michael Coady

---

[1] The Wren's Burial
[2] The White Deal Board' : 18th - Century love song
[3] And let us say no more of that' : refrain of Ballad The Limerick Rake

Hartnett Abú

Instinct, intelligence and wit
drove your restless spirit.
In truth, a man needs little more.

The enemy of injustice, you strove
to turn bad to good, good to better.
Few could do it so well —

exposing hypocrisy and fakery
yet never neglecting to celebrate
the world's unbridled beauty.

Hartnett, abú! Although words
no longer flow from your deft hand
your light continues to stray across

this universe and expand, expand, expand.

Martin Vaughan

The True Poet Beckons Forever

Your pony grazed a long acre of grass
that reached no cross or finish;
whitethorn blossom was a thin money
that you bruised with a pinch.

Even when the wind was dry
or the sun was alight,
you had rain in your pockets,
rain in your mind.

In your coat of blackbirds
you were the tune in the hedge.
When you were gone, gone,

you were never dead.
Your shoes of grass await in the grass
for those who step where you stepped.

John W. Sexton

Ceist agus freagra éigin na teanga
I gcuimhne Michael Hartnett

Is ainnis mo theach
taobh le fothrach.

Ach tá deis agam
rogha agam
bheith ar an seachrán
agus puball a chur suas in aon áit is ansa liom

cois abhainn b'fhéidir
atá ag bogadh
go séimh
go domhain.

Ní h-í an ailtireacht atá igceist
ach nasc
caidreamh.

Carmel Cummins

The Legacy of a Poet
in memory of Michael Hartnett

You have gone into the realm of memory
All the age old demons that taunted you
Are silent,

I conjure up the cadence of your speech
Think of the time you arrived
In a borrowed suit

And sought an advance of fees
To buy a disposable razor,
There was a poem there somewhere.

And later in the fullness of Guinness
You read from an inspiring repertoire
And we were stunned.

The words that flowed with ease
Are now stilled;
I read them yet
And hear your voice, the legacy of a poet.

Gearoid O'Brien

"After life's fitful fever...

Her honey hair, her eyes/Small ovals of thrush-eggs...
he willed to me his bitterness and thirst/
his cold ability to close a door...
in a stone-cold kitchen
she clenched her brittle hands
around a world/she could not understand.

Better than a prize, festivals or bronze
Some poems live on in glorious company.

...he sleeps well". *Macbeth* III, ii, 25

John Pinschmidt

Hartnett Laudation

Through his death I realize
how I value poetry.
O hut of our mystery, emptied
and isolated always.

Ó hAirtnéide is dead.

Poetry is daunted.
A stave of the barrel is smashed
and the wall of learning broken.

Seamus Heaney

Note: Translation & Adaptation of Tadhg O h-Uiginn.

Extract from 'Hartnett Laudation' given at Michael Hartnett's Memorial Service, Dublin, October 1999.

Hagiography

Just back from Éigse Michael Hartnett.
You'd have to laugh. Your corpse not even cold yet.

Very aboriginal to be beneath a sign at the brand new estate:
Address — Michael Hartnett Close, Newcastle West.

Its position is perfect — right opposite Coole Lane.
Stood there in the pouring rain with your son

Across from The Healing Streams Therapy Centre,
St Vincent de Paul, within earshot of the river

On a quiet day.
Get this: the story Joan Mac Kernan
Told us of the poetry workshop for children

Earlier, when she asked who'd heard of Michael Hartnett,
The lad who cried 'Miss, Miss, I live in Michael Hartnett.'

I recognised the mantra
Like a glittering speck of mica

Whirling down the bardos from another incarnation
And the flash of recognition has it graven on my brain.

All together now: I live in Michael Hartnett.
I live in Michael Hartnett. I live in Michael Hartnett.

Paula Meehan

Michael Hartnett Chronology

1941- Born September 18th in Croom maternity hospital Limerick. Eldest child of Denis and Bridie Harnett, registrar incorrectly records birth as 'Hartnett'

1942- Infant brother Edward dies aged 6 weeks

1944- Fostered out to native Irish speaker maternal grandmother Bridget O'Halpin

1948- Moves back to family home in Maiden Street Newcastle West, begins school.

1951- 3 year old sister Patricia dies.

1961- Completes Leaving Certificate, moves to London works as a tea boy for a short period, moves back to Limerick. Works as postman, co-writes a play *An Lasair Choille* with then girlfriend Caitlín Maude

1962- *Poetry Ireland* debuts Hartnett, publishing three of his poems. In autumn he enrols in U.C.D on a scholarship studying Latin, Philosophy, English and Economics. *Tao: A Version of the Chinese Classic of the Sixth Century,* is published as a supplement in *Arena* literary magazine.

1966- In London, he marries Rosemary Grantley

1968- Dolmen Press publish first collection *Anatomy of a Cliché*. Daughter Lara born, family move to Dublin from London.

1969- New Island press publish *The Hag of Beare.*

1970- *Selected Poems* published by New Writer's Press

1973- *Gypsy Ballads: A Version of the Romancero Gitano of Frederico Garcia Lorca* published by Goldsmith Press.

1974- On the stage of the Peacock Theatre Dublin, he announces intention to stop writing poetry in English. The Hartnett family move to Glendarragh, Templeglantine in rural west Limerick.

1975- *A Farewell to English* is published by Gallery Press. First bilingual collection - *The Retreat of Ita Cagney:* Cúlú íde published by Goldsmith Press.

1977- *Poems in English* published by Dolmen Press, *Prisoners* published by the Gallery Press.

1978- *Adharca Broic* published by Gallery Press

1980- Wins the Irish-American Cultural Institute award.

1983- *An Phurgóid* published by Coiscéim.

1984- Marriage with Rosemary breaks down, he leaves family home moves to Inchicore Dublin.

1985- *Inchicore Haiku* published, marks a return to new work being published in the English language. *Collected Poems Volume 1* published by Raven Arts Press/ Carcanet Press. *An Lia Nocht* published by Coiscéim. Translation of Dáithí Ó Bruadair (1623-1698), *O Bruadair* published by the Gallery Press.

1986- Wins the Arts Council/an Chomhairle Ealaíon award for best book in Irish.

1987- The bi-lingual collection *A Necklace of Wrens* published by the Gallery Press.

1988- Receives the Irish American Cultural Institute award. *Poems to Younger Women* published by the Gallery Press.

1990- The American Fund Literary Award.

1992- *The Killing of Dreams* published by Gallery Press.

1993- *Haicéad*, a translation of the poetry of Pádraigín Haicéad (1600 -1654).

1994- *Selected and New Poems* published by Gallery Press 1994.

1998- *O Rathaille: Translations from the Irish, of Aodhagan O Rathaille (c.1670-1729)* is published by Gallery Press.

1999- Documentary on Michael Hartnett's life *A Necklace of Wrens*, (directed by Pat Collins) is released.
Michael dies in a Dublin hospital on the 13 October from alcoholic liver syndrome aged 58.

2000- The annual Éigse Michael Hartnett Literary and Arts Festival launched in Newcastle West.

2001- *Collected Poems* published by Gallery Press to mark Michael's 60th year.

2002- *A Book of Strays*, edited by Peter Fallon published by Gallery Press.

2003- *Translations*, edited by Peter Fallon published by Gallery Press.

2006- A book of critical essays *Remembering Michael Hartnett* published by Four Courts Press edited by Stephen Newman and John McDonagh.

2009- Niall Hartnett publishes a book of stories, poetry and photographs *Notes From His Contemporaries: A Tribute to Michael Hartnett*.

2011- A life sized statue of Michael unveiled in his native town by poet Paul Durcan commissioned by Newcastle West Community Council and sculpted by Rory Breslin.

2012- A biography of Michael *A Rebel Act: Michael Hartnett's Farewell to English* written by Pat Walsh is published by Mercier Press.

2013- A book of poems in celebration of Michael, *I Live in Michael Hartnett* is published by Revival Press / The Limerick Writers' Centre in association with County Limerick Arts Office and edited by James Lawlor.

Acknowledgements

The editor James Lawlor would like to thank all the poets who have contributed to this anthology. I would also like to thank Dominic Taylor of The Limerick Writers' Centre who originally approached me with the idea of this book and has been a constant source of advice. I would particularly like to thank Joan Mac Kernan for her belief in the project and for always bringing her knowledge, expertise and vision to the table. Sincere thanks to all those who provided advice and encouragement especially Niall Hartnett and the Hartnett estate, Theo Dorgan, Peter Fallon, Nuala Ní Dhomhnaill, Mike Mac Domhnaill, graphic designer Jason Cooke, Tony Curtis, Pat Boran and Eileen Sheehan.

We would also like to thank all the publishers who gave permission for the use of texts; The Gallery Press, Jonathan Cape Ltd, Dedalus Press, Bloodaxe Books, Carcanet Press, The Harvill Press, Mercier Press, New Island, Riposte Books, Doghouse Books and Arlen House. The copyright remains with the respective authors, I have been asked by the following publishers to provide supplementary information for which I am glad to oblige.

'Adhlacadh an Dreoilín' and 'Twenty-four Hours from Tulla' - By Michael Coady By kind permission of the author and The Gallery Press, Loughcrew, Oldcastle, County Meath, Ireland from *One Another* (2003)

'End' by Peter Fallon- By kind permission of the author and The Gallery Press, Loughcrew, Oldcastle, County Meath, Ireland from *The Company of Horses* (2007)

'Michael and the Angel' by Eiléan Ní Chuilleanáin -By kind permission of the author and The Gallery Press, Loughcrew, Oldcastle, County Meath, Ireland from *The Sun-fish* (2009)

'O Winged Bird' by John Liddy – By kind permission of the author and Revival Press from *The Well: New and Selected Poems* (2007)

'Michael Hartnett, The Poet King' by Paul Durcan –By kind permission of the author and Harvill Press from *The Art of Life* (2004)

'So What If There's No Happy Endings' by Gabriel Fitzmaurice – By kind permission of the author and Mercier Press from *The Essential Gabriel Fitzmaurice* (2008) © Gabriel Fitzmaurice

'An October Sun' by Michael Longley – By kind permission of the author and Jonathan Cape Ltd from *Snow Water* (2004)

'Missing You' by Rita Kelly – By kind permission of the author and Arlen House, Galway from *Travelling West* (2000)

'Final Version' by Paddy Bushe –By kind permission of author and Dedalus Press.

'The Princess of Sorrows' by Pat Boran -By kind permission of author and Dedalus Press.

'Michael Michael' by Theo Dorgan –By kind permission of author and Dedalus Press.

Leland Bardwell 'The Act of Poetry is a Rebel Act' -By kind permission of author and Dedalus Press.

'West Going West' by Macdara Woods -By kind permission of author and Dedalus Press.

'Hagiography' by Paula Meehan -By kind permission of author and Carcanet Press from Painting Rain *(2009)* 'Hagiography' first published it in an anthology by Errigal Writers.

'Irish Poetry' by Eavan Boland –By kind permission of author and Carcanet Press.

Every effort has been made to trace copyright holders and to obtain their permission for the use of copyright material. The publisher apologizes for any errors or omissions in the above list and would be grateful if notified of any corrections that should be incorporated in future reprints or editions of this book.

The Contributors

Eavan Boland was born in Dublin (1944) and was educated in T.C.D. Her poetry collections have won many awards include a Lannan Foundation Award in Poetry and an American Ireland Fund Literary Award. She also received the Corrington Medal for Literary Excellence Centenary College 2002, the Bucknell Medal of Distinction 2000 Bucknell University, the Smartt Family prize from the Yale Review and the John Frederick Nims Award from Poetry Magazine 2002. Since 1996, she has been a tenured Professor of English at Stanford University where she is currently Bella Mabury and Eloise Mabury Knapp Professor in the Humanities and Melvin and Bill Lane Professor for Director of the Creative Writing program.

Pat Boran was born in Portlaoise, Ireland in 1963 and currently lives in Dublin. He has published four full-length collections of poetry as well as a New and Selected volume. Those books are: *The Unwound Clock* (1990), which won the Patrick Kavanagh Award, *Familiar Things* (1993), *The Shape of Water* (1996) and *As the Hand, the Glove* (2001). His *New and Selected Poems,* with an introduction by Dennis O'Driscoll, was published in 2005 and reissued by Dedalus in 2007. His new collection, *The Next Life,* was published by Dedalus in 2012. A former editor of Poetry Ireland Review and presenter of The Poetry Programme on RTÉ Radio 1, he has edited many anthologies of poetry, among them *Wingspan: A Dedalus Sampler* (2006), *Flowing, Still: Irish Poets on Irish Poetry* (2009), *The Bee-Loud Glade* (2009) and *Shine On,* in support of mental ill health. A member of Aosdána, he received the Lawrence O'Shaughnessy Poetry Award in 2008.

Paddy Bushe was born in Dublin in 1948. A poet who writes in both English and Irish, he has published many poetry collections, among them *Poems With Amergin* (Beaver Row Press, 1989), *Teanga* (Coiscéim, 1990), *Counsellor* (Sceilg Press, 1991), *Digging Towards The Light* (Dedalus Press, 1994), *In Ainneoin na gCloch* (Coiscéim, 2001), *Hopkins on Skellig Michael* (Dedalus Press, 2001), *The Nitpicking of Cranes* (Dedalus, 2004) and, most recently, *To Ring in Deadalus* (Dedalus Press, 2007).The recipient of the Oireachtas prize for poetry in 2006, Paddy Bushe was also the recipient of the 2006 Michael Hartnett Poetry Award. He lives in Co. Kerry and is a member of Aosdána

Leland Bardwell is a poet, novelist and playwright, born in India of Irish parents in 1922. Her family returned to Ireland in 1924 settling in Co. Kildare, Leland was educated in Dublin. Her poetry collections include *The Mad Cyclist* (1970), *The Fly and the Bedbug* (1984), *Dostoevsky's Grave/New and Selected Poems* (1991) and the *White Beach* (1998), *The Noise of Masonry Settling* (2006). Her novels are *Girl on a Bicycle* (1977), *That London Winter* (1981), *The House* (1984), *There We Have Been* (1989) and *Mother to a Stranger* (2002, trans. German). Short story collection: *Different Kinds of Love* (1986 trans. German and French). Her plays include *The Life of Edith Piaf,* Olympia (1985). *Open Ended Prescription,* Peacock, and BBC Radio, *Jocasta* and *Also on the Rocks* Other plays for BBC and radio plus some children's plays for RTÉ. Leland won the Marten Toonder Award in 1992 and is a founding editor of the literary journal, Cyphers. She now lives in Co. Sligo where she founded the annual literary festival, Scriobh. She is a member of Aosdána.

Cathy Bryant is a writer and poet. Her poems and stories have been published all over the world and she's won numerous awards. She co-edits the annual anthology *Best of Manchester Poets,* and her collection *Contains Strong Language and Scenes of a Sexual Nature* was published by Puppywolf in 2010.

Siobhan Campbell is on the faculty at Kingston University London where she lectures on the low-residency MFA in Creative Writing. Her latest book is Cross-Talk (Seren Books), 'set in the wake of the turbulent Irish peace process' - Poetry. She is widely anthologised, including in the Field Day Anthology of Irish Literature (NYU Press). Identity Parade, New British and Irish Poets (Bloodaxe) and Womens' Work: Two Centuries of writing by women (Seren). Her work appears regularly in the US, the UK and Ireland with publication in *The Southern Review, Crab Orchard Review, Poetry, Magma, Agenda, Poetry Ireland etc.* An award winner in the National Poetry Competition, the Troubadour International and the Templar Pamphlet competition she lives in London.

Eileen Casey received a Katherine Kavanagh Fellowship in 2011. Her poetry books include *Drinking the Colour Blue* (New Island), *From Bone to Blossom* (Altents Publishing) and *Seagulls.* Originally from the Midlands she lives in Tallaght. She was a visiting writer, with support from Culture Ireland, on the Eastern Washington University's Winter Programme, Lexington, Kentucky, 2011. Her work is widely published in outlets such as Poetry Ireland Review, The Ulster Tatler, Abridged, among others. Awards include The Oliver Goldsmith International Prize, The Moore Medallion, The Scottish International Poetry Award, among others.

Michael Coady is a member of Aosdána and has published five books with The Gallery Press, the most recent being GOING BY WATER. He lives in Carrick-on-Suir, Co. Tipperary, where he was born. The winner of a number of literary prizes and awards, he held the Heimbold chair in Irish Studies at Villanova University, Pennsylvania, in 2005, and a residency at the Irish Cultural Centre, Paris, in 2008.

Declan Collinge is a bi-lingual poet and critic. To date he has published two collections in English and three in Irish. A new collection 'The Lonely Hush of Eve' Selected and New Poems is due for publication by Mentor Books later this year. He was a contributor 'Remembering Michael Hartnett' (Four Courts Press, 2006).

Anthony Cronin was born in Enniscorthy, County Wexford in 1928. He is a poet, critic, and novelist. His first collection Poems was published by Cresset in 1958 (London). He was visiting lecturer at the University of Montana 1966-68 and poet in residence at Drake University (1968-70). He was a *Irish Times* columnist with a weekly discourse, *'Viewpoint'* (1974-80). A biographer of Brian O'Nolan and Samuel Beckett, Anthony was cultural and artistic adviser to former Taoiseach, Charles J. Haughey as well as part of a small group who organised the first ever Bloomsday celebration. He also produced television programmes incl. 'Between Two Canals' and 'Flann O'Brien - Man of Parts'. He lives in Dublin and contributes to the *Sunday Independent*. In 1983 he received the Marten Toonder Award (1983) for his contribution to Irish literature. He is a founding member of Aosdána and was elected Saoi of Aosdána in 2003 and is a member of its governing body, the Toscaireacht.

Rugadh **Carmel Cummins** i gContae Chill Chainnigh agus tá sí ina cónaí ann. Tá a cuid filíochta i mBéarla foilsithe in irisí náisiúnta agus í mbailiúcháin ó Chill Chainnigh *(Kilkenny Anthology, Ink Bottle, new writings from Kilkenny, Woodstock Promenade, Kilkenny Broadsheets)* agus a prós i *Townlands: a habitation*. Is é seo an chéad dán i nGaeilge atá foilithe aici.

Tony Curtis was born in Dublin in 1955. He studied literature at Essex University and Trinity College Dublin. An award winning poet, Curtis has published eight warmly received collections. In 2003 he was awarded the Varuna House Exchange Fellowship to Australia. Curtis has been awarded the Irish National Poetry Prize. In 2008, *Days Like These* (with Theo Dorgan & Paula Meehan) was published by Brooding Heron Press. His new collections *Folk* (Arc Publications), *An Elephant Called Rex and a Dog Called Dumbo* (Black Hills Press) with illustrations by Pat Mooney from N.C.A.D., *and Sand Works* (Real Ireland) with Irish photographer Liam Blake, were all recently published. He is a member of Aosdana.

Pádraig J. Daly: Born, Dungarvan, Co. Waterford, 1943. Augustinian friar. Working in a Dublin parish. His tenth collection, *"AfterLife"*, was published by Dedalus in 2010. His previous collection *"Clinging to the Myth"* came in 2007. He has also published several volumes of translations from Irish and from Italian. Translations of his poetry have been made into several European languages.

Greg Delanty was born in Cork, Ireland in 1958, and now lives for most of the year in America, where he teaches at St Michael's College, Vermont. His earlier books include *Cast in the Fire* (1986), *Southward* (1992), *American Wake* (1995) and *The Hellbox* (1998). He was awarded the Austin Clarke Centenary Poetry award in 1996 and won the National Poetry Competition in 1999. He has also received numerous other awards including the Patrick Kavanagh Poetry Award (1983), the Allen Dowling Poetry Fellowship (1986), the Wolfers-O'Neill Award (1996–97), an Arts Council of Ireland Bursary (1998–99), an award from the Royal Literary Fund (1999), and a Guggenheim Fellowship.

Theo Dorgan was born in Cork in 1953. He is a poet, prose writer, documentary screenwriter, editor, translator and broadcaster. His poetry collections are *The Ordinary House of Love, Rosa Mundi* and *Sappho's Daughter, What This Earth Cost Us* and *Greek*. His prose account of a transatlantic crossing under sail, *Sailing For Home,* was published by in

2004. In the same year, his libretto *Jason And The Argonauts*, to music by Howard Goodall, was commissioned by and premiered at The Royal Albert Hall, London. A further prose book, *Time On The Ocean, A Voyage from Cape Horn to Cape Town*, was published by New Island in 2010. He has also edited a number of books, his latest being *The Book of Uncommon Prayer*. A former Director of Poetry Ireland/Éigse Éireann, he has worked extensively as a broadcaster of literary programmes on both radio and television. He was presenter of Poetry Now on RTÉ Radio 1, and later presented RTÉ's TV books programme, Imprint. Among his awards are the Listowel Prize for Poetry, 1992, and The O'Shaughnessy Prize For Irish Poetry 2010. A member of Aosdána, he served on The Arts Council / An Chomhairle Ealaíon 2003 -2008. He lives in Dublin.

Oliver Dunne has contributed illustrations to *Hot Press* and *The Sunday Independent*, in the Republic of Ireland, and Punch, magazine and website, in England. As well as in a variety of periodicals, his poems have appeared in the anthologies *Lifelines 2* (TownHouse 1994), *Human Rights Have No Borders: Voices of Irish Poets* (Marino 1998) and *New and Collected Lifelines* (TownHouse 2006). His poetry was also included in the landmark anthology of Irish poetry, the 100th issue of Poetry Ireland Review (March 2010), edited by Paul Muldoon.

Seán Dunne (1956-1995) was a poet born in Waterford, Ireland. He edited several anthologies, beginning with *The Poets of Munster* (1985) and finishing with the *Ireland Anthology* which was completed posthumously by George O'Brien and his partner Trish Edelstein. He released 3 collections of poems. Seán Dunne's collections of poems have all been well received, and in order of release are: *Against the Storm* (1985), *The Sheltered Nest* (1992) and *Time and the Island*. The account of his childhood *"In My Father's House"* was released in 1991, and was a bestseller. An annual festival is held in his honour in his native city of Waterford.

Paul Durcan was born in Dublin in 1944, he studied Archaeology and Medieval History at University College Cork. His first solo collection of poetry, *O Westport in the Light of Asia Minor*, won the Patrick Kavanagh Award in 1975; later collections include *Teresa's Bar* (1976), *Sam's Cross* (1978), *Ark of the North* (1982), *Jesus, Break his Fall* (1983), and *Going Home to Russia* (1987). *The Berlin Wall Café* (1985) was a choice of the London Poetry Book Society, and *Daddy, Daddy* (1990) won the Whitbread Poetry Prize. More recently he published *Crazy About Women* (1991), *Give Me Your Hand* (1994), *Christmas Day* (1996), *Greetings to Our Friends in Brazil* (1999), *Cries of an Irish Caveman* (2001) *The Art of Life* (2004) *The laughter of our Mothers* (2007) *Life is A Dream: 40 Years Reading Poems* (2009) and *Praise in Which I Live and Move and Have My Being* (2012). He is Ireland Professor of Poetry 2004-2007. He is a member of Aosdána and lives in Dublin.

Desmond Egan's latest Collection (of over 10 books) is 'Hopkins in Kildare'. He has published two widely-praised Prose Collections; two direct Translations of Greek plays. His Poetry has been published in book form in 21 languages and he has been awarded an Hon. Doctorate by Washburn

University. Full-time writer; Artistic Director of the G.M. Hopkins Festival, now 25 years old.

Peter Fallon was born in Germany in 1951 and grew up on his uncle's farm near Kells in County Meath. He is an Honours Graduate of Trinity College, Dublin, where he has been Writer Fellow and Visiting Writer in the English Department. At the age of eighteen he founded The Gallery Press which has published more than four hundred books of poems and plays by Ireland's finest established and emerging authors and which is recognized internationally as the country's pre-eminent literary publishing house. Among the writers it publishes are Derek Mahon, John Montague, Nuala Ní Dhomhnaill, Ciaran Carson, Medbh McGuckian, John Banville, Eiléan Ní Chuilleanáin and Michael Hartnett. His own collections of poems include *The Speaking Stones* (1978), *Winter Work* (1983), *The News and Weather* (1987) and *Eye to Eye* (1992). His selected poems, *News of the World,* was published in the US by Wake Forest University Press in 1993. An expanded edition, *News of the World: Selected and New Poems,* was published in Ireland in 1998, included in the Irish Times' 'Books of the Year', and reprinted twice. His poems have been translated into French, German, Irish and Japanese and volumes of Selected Poems have been published in Romanian and Hungarian. He is a member of Aosdána.

Pauline Fayne was born in Dublin in 1954. Her poems have been published in a variety of magazines and anthologies in Ireland and have been broadcast on radio stations throughout Europe. Her first three collections *'Journey'* (Sheveck Press 1979), *'Killer of Fishes'* (Stonebridge Publications 2001), and *'I'm Fine, Really'* (Stonebridge Publications 2005) are now out of print. Her New and Selected poems *'Mowing in the dark'* was published by *Revival Press* in June 2011. An interview and a selection of her poems can be heard on www.podcasts.ie.

Huib Fens was born in 1954. An Artist and, poet, graduate of the Tilburg Art School and the Royal College of Arts in Den Bosch. Professor at Fontys College of Art Tilburg. Formed the Factories Photography Project with R. van den Bergh in 1997. Worked as editor at Wagner&VanSanten Poetry Publishers. Founded de Aalse Pers Publishers in 2010. (Belgium) www.huibfens.be www.factories.nl

Marian Finan Hewitt was born in county Roscommon. Now living in Dublin. She has been published in newspapers, magazines, periodicals and workshop collections.

Gabriel Fitzmaurice was born in Co. Kerry in 1952. He is a Bilingual poet, literary advisor, translator, teacher, musician, broadcaster. In addition to broadcasting on Irish radio and television, Fitzmaurice has written extensively in English and Irish. Among his English poetry collections are *Rainsong, Road to the Horizon, Dancing Through, The Father's Part* and *The Village Sings*. In Irish, he has published the collection *Nocht*. A primary school teacher, Fitzmaurice is also the author of the children's verse collection, *The Moving Stair*. He works as a translator of essays and collections of songs/ballads from the original Irish and has twice represented Ireland at the European Festival of Poetry. Along with writing and teaching,

Fitzmaurice has found success as a singer of traditional Irish music. He resides in Kerry.

Rody Gorman was born in Dublin, Ireland in 1960 and now lives in the Isle of Skye, Scotland. He has published many collections of poetry in English, Irish and Scottish Gaelic. His selected poems in Irish and Scottish Gaelic, Chernilo, were published by Coiscéim in 2006. He has worked as writing fellow at Sabhal Mòr Ostaig, University College Cork and the University of Manitoba and is editor of the annual Irish and Scottish Gaelic poetry anthology An Guth. He has worked as Convenor of the Translation and Linguistic Rights Committee of Scottish PEN; Chair of HI-Arts Writing Development Group, as Specialist Adviser for the Scottish Arts Council, and as songwriter, lecturer, creative writing tutor and adjudicator of literary competitions.

Joe Healy is a resident of West Limerick. Joe currently works as a technician in the councils transport department and lives near the village of Kilmeedy, County Limerick. He has enjoyed reading his work at venues such as the White House and Lock Bar public houses in Limerick City, also in many venues across Munster. Previous work has been published by Soft Newsletter, Weekly Observer Newspapers and Revival Press. In December 2010 Joe was featured in Sextet – A Revival Poetry Anthology.

Louise Hegarty is 23 years old and lives in Cork. She has previously won the Yeats Emerging Writer Poetry Competition 2009 and a Poetry Award at Listowel Writers' Week. Most recently she was shortlisted for the inaugural RTE Guide/Penguin Ireland short story competition. I have work published or forthcoming in *Wordlegs, The Poetry Bus* magazine, *Minus 9 Squared, Popshot Magazine, Crannóg, Boyne Berries, Thefirstcut and Cuadrivio*.

Seamus Heaney was born in Co. Derry in 1939, he studied at Queen's University, Belfast. His major poetry collections include *Death of a Naturalist* (1966), Door Into the Dark (1969), *Wintering Out* (1972), *North* (1975), *Field Work* (1979), *Station Island* (1984), *The Haw Lantern* (1987), which won the Whitbread Poetry Award, *Seeing Things* (1991), *Electric Light* (2001) and *District and Circle* (2006). *The Spirit Level* (1996) and his translation of *Beowulf* (1999) both won the Whitbread Book of the Year Award. He has published several works of prose and criticism, including *Preoccupations* (1980), *The Government of the Tongue* (1988) and *The Redress of Poetry* (1995). He has done translations of two plays, *The Cure at Troy: A Version of Sophocles' Philoctetes* (1990) and *The Burial at Thebes: A Version of Sophocles' Antigone* (2005), and co-edited two selections of poetry with Ted Hughes, *The Rattle Bag* (1982) and *The School Bag* (1997). He taught English and poetry at Queen's University and at Harvard University, and was professor of poetry at Oxford University from 1989 to 1994. He won the Nobel Prize for Literature in 1995. He was elected Saoi of Aosdána in 1997. He lives in Dublin.

Eleanor Hooker lives in North Tipperary. She has a BA (Hons 1st) from the Open University, an MA (Hons.) in Cultural History from the University of Northumbria, and an MPhil in Creative Writing (Distinction) from Trinity

College, Dublin. She was selected for the Poetry Ireland Introductions Series in 2011. Her poetry has been published in journals in Ireland and the UK. She is a founding member, Vice-Chairperson and PRO for the Dromineer Literary Festival. She is a helm and Press Officer for the Lough Derg RNLI Lifeboat. She began her career as a nurse and midwife. *The Shadow Owner's Companion (Dedalus Press)* is her debut collection of poems.

Leonard Holman has had poems published in *The Stony Thursday* and Revival literary magazine. His short stories have appeared in the *Limerick Leader, Christmas Gazette* and the *Limerick Chronicle*. He has self published a book of short stories entitled *The Dark Horse Stories*. He lives in Limerick.

Joseph Horgan was born in Birmingham, England, of Irish parents. He is a poet, author, journalist, and reviewer. His writings and poems have appeared in numerous literary journals in Ireland, the UK, Europe and America and have been broadcast on television and radio. He is a past winner of The Patrick Kavanagh Award. He has been a recipient of an Arts Council bursary and a Cork County Council Arts bursary. His first collection of poetry, *Slipping Letters Beneath the Sea,* was published by Doghouse in 2008. His book, *The Song at Your Backdoor,* a meditation on identity and place, was published by Collins Press in 2010. It was selected as an RTE Book on One. He has previously been chosen for the Poetry Ireland Introduction Series. He has been a visiting writer at the Irish Writers in London Summer School. He writes a weekly column for the Irish Post.

Fred Johnston was born in Belfast, Northern Ireland, in 1951, educated there and in Toronto, Canada. Novelist, poet and critic, he was Writer-in-Residence at the Princess Grace Irish Library, Monaco, in the Autumn of 2004. He is the founder of Galway's annual literature festival, Cúirt and of its writers' centre and translates contemporary French poetry. He lives and works in Galway.

Rita Kelly was born in Galway in 1953. She is writer of poetry, fiction, drama and criticism, in both English and Irish. She has won various awards for her work, including the Sean Ó Riordain Oireachtas Award; an Irish Times Poetry Award; Maxwell House Award. Her work has been translated into German, Italian, French and Dutch.

Brendan Kennelly (born 1936) is a prolific and fluent writer, with more than twenty books of poems to his credit, including *My Dark Fathers* (1964), *Collection One: Getting Up Early* (1966), *Good Souls to Survive* (1967), *Dream of a Black Fox* (1968), *Love Cry* (1972), *The Voices* (1973). He is also the author of two novels, *"The Crooked Cross"* (1963) and *"The Florentines"* (1967), and three plays in a Greek Trilogy, He was Professor of Modern Literature at Trinity College Dublin until 2005. He is now retired and occasionally tours the USA as university lecturer.

Mae Leonard is originally from Limerick, now living in Kildare. For many years she has been broadcast regularly on RTE Radio One's, .Sunday Miscellany programme. Her poetry collection, I Shouldn't be Telling you This, was published by DOGHOUSE in 2011.

John Liddy, born in Youghal, County Cork, but raised in Limerick, is a poet whose collections include *Boundaries* (1974), *The Angling Cot* (1991), *Song of the Empty Cage* (1997, Lawping Press), and *Wine and Hope/Vino y Esperanza* (1999, Archione Editorial Madrid), *Cast-a-Net* (2003, Archione Editorial Madrid), *The Well: New and Selected Poems* (2007, Revival Press). Most recent book is *Gleanings* (2010, Revival Press). He co-founded The Stony Thursday Book with Jim Burke and edits occasional issues. Liddy currently lives in Madrid, where he works as a teacher/librarian. He also runs the annual poetry festival An Tobar/El Manantial, along with Matthew Loughney and the Embassy of Ireland.

Michael Longley CBE was born in Belfast in 1939 and educated at the Royal Belfast Academical Institution and Trinity College Dublin. He worked as a teacher, and served as director of literature and traditional arts for the Arts Council of Northern Ireland from 1970 to 1991. His books of poetry include *No Continuing City* (1969), *An Exploded View* (1973), *Man Lying on a Wall* (1976), *The Echo Gate* (1979), *The Ghost Orchid* (1995), which was short-listed for the T.S. Eliot Award. *Gorse Fires* won the Whitbread Poetry Prize in 1991, and *The Weather in Japan* won the Irish Times Literature Prize for Poetry, the Hawthornden Prize and the T.S. Eliot Prize in 2001. He published an autobiographical work, *Tuppeny Stung,* in 1994, and he has edited selections of poems by Louis MacNeice and W. R. Rodgers. Other awards include the Irish-American Cultural Institute Award and the Eric Gregory Award, which he shared with Derek Mahon in 1965. In 2001, he was awarded the Queen's Gold Medal for Poetry. He is a fellow of the Royal Society of Literature, and was appointed to the Ireland Chair of Poetry in 2007; a professorship he has held for the three years. He lives in Belfast with his wife, the distinguished critic and editor Edna Longley, Professor Emerita at Queen's University. He is a member of Aosdána.

Gerald Lyne is a former Keeper of Manuscripts at the National Library of Ireland, an economic and social historian, Kerry and west Cork, 1650-1850 and poet. His book on *William Steuart Trench, Agent of the Lansdowne Estate in Kerry, 1849 -72* (Dublin, 2001) was awarded the National University of Ireland Historical Prize for Best Historical Research in 2001.

Tom Matthews was born in Dublin in 1952. After working in advertising he studied Fine Art at the National College of Art and Design in Dublin. He has been a freelance cartoonist, writer and critic since 1975. His work appears weekly in *The Irish Times* and *Sunday Independent*. He has had thirty one-man shows and his paintings have been exhibited in Living Art, the National Portrait Show and at the RHA. He has illustrated a dozen books, written a novel and published three volumes of cartoons. His last book, The New Adventures of Keats and Chapman, was published in 2008. His first poetry collection *The Owl and the Pussycat* was published by Dedalus Press in 2009

Catherine Phil MacCarthy's fourth collection, *The Invisible Threshold* is due from Dedalus Press, Dublin in September. She won the Fish International Poetry Prize in 2010 and is a former editor of *Poetry Ireland Review*.

Mike Mac Domhnaill is a poet and community activist, born in 1953 at Clouncagh, County Limerick his family moved to Newcastle West in 1957 after his father's death. The poems in his book *Widow's Son/Mac Baintrí* reflect on locality, history, nature, family, world, belief. He has been published in various journals, he was short-listed for the Francis Mac Manus Short Story Award 2007 and has work read on RTE Radio 1 during the summer of 2009. His latest collection *Macalla Maidu,* published by Coisceim will be launched at Éigse Michael Hartnett 2013.

Hugh McFadden was born in Derry, lived briefly there and in Donegal, before moving to Dublin. For many years he was a journalist and regularly reviewed books for the Press Group of papers, as well as for *Hibernia* magazine, *The Irish Independent, The Irish Times* and *The Sunday Tribune.* McFadden was also a history researcher with The Irish Manuscripts Commission and an editorial assistant on *The Correspondence of Daniel O'Connell* (IUP–Blackwater Press/ 8 vols.). He is the executor of the literary estate of the writer John Jordan and has edited, with an introduction, Jordan's *Selected Poems,* which was published by Dedalus Press in April 2008. Three collections of his own poems have been published, the most recent being *Elegies and Epiphanies: Selected Poems* (Lagan Press, Belfast, 2005). His own previous collections are: *Cities of Mirrors* (Beaver Row Press, Dublin, 1984) and *Pieces of Time* (Lapwing Publications, Belfast, 2004).

B.D.MacMahon is a photographer and marine environmentalist living in Mystic, Connecticut with family roots in Clare. www.bdmacmahon.com

Paula Meehan was born in Dublin in 1955. She studied at Trinity College, Dublin and at Eastern Washington University in the United States. She has published six collections of poetry. She has also written plays for both adults and children. She has conducted residencies in universities, in prisons, in the wider community, and her poems and plays have been translated into many languages, including Irish. Recent collections are *Dharmakaya* and *Painting Rain,* from Carcanet Press, Manchester and from Wake Forest University Press, North Carolina. *Music for Dog* a collection of award-winning radio plays is available from Dedalus Press, Dublin, who have also reissued *Mysteries of the Home,* a selection of seminal work from the 1980s and 1990s. Among other awards, she has received the Butler Literary Award for Poetry presented by the Irish American Cultural Institute, the Marten Toonder Award for Literature, and the Denis Devlin Award. A collection of critical essays on her poetry and plays was published as a special issue by the U.S. journal An Sionnach. She lives in Dublin and is a member of Aosdána.

Hayden Murphy (born 1945) is an Irish editor and poet. Born in Dublin, and brought up there and in Limerick, he was educated at Blackrock College and Trinity College, Dublin. During 1967-78 he edited, published, and personally distributed Broadsheet, which contained poetry and graphics.

Teri Murray has been living in Limerick for many years as a poet, editor, novelist and playwright. Her fourth poetry collection, *Where the Daghda Dances: New and Selected Poems,* was published most recently (Revival

Press, 2010), preceded by *Coddle and Tripe* (Stonebridge, 1998), a joint book with her partner, the late Limerick poet Liam Mulligan, *Poems from the Exclusion Zone* (Stonebridge, 2001), and *The Authority of Winter* (Stonebridge, 2007). Other notable works include *A Time Under Heaven*, her play about the history of Limerick, staged at the Belltable in 1996, and a book for children, *Eddy the Teddy and the Big Fat Nana*, in 2003. Murray was editor for Scratches on the Wall, an anthology of Limerick writers from Tholsel Press, 1995, and is former editor of the Revival Literary Journal.

Christopher Murray is a retired professor of English. He taught at University College Dublin for many years, as well as the University of New Haven, University of Antwerp, Waseda University- Tokyo and the University of Pecs- Hungary. He is widely published as a literary critic as well as editing *Beckett at 100: Centenary Essays* (2006, New Island Press Dublin). A book of poetry entitled *Vanishings* is pending from Salmon.

Caitríona Ní Chléirchín is originally from Gortmoney, Emyvale in Co. Monaghan. She is an Irish-language lecturer in University College Dublin and is completing a doctorate on the poetry of Nuala Ní Dhomhnaill and Biddy Jenkinson at present. She spent a year in Lyon, France studying masters in French literature and was very influenced by *écriture féminine*. She gives voice to the feminine speaking subject in her poetry. Mícheál Ó Ruairc has described her as the new love lyricist writing Irish poetry today in *Comhar*, December 2010. *Crithloinnir* her début collection of poetry won first prize in the Oireachtas competition for new writers in 2010. She has published poetry in *Comhar, Feasta* and *Blaiseadh Pinn, Cyphers, The Shop, An t-Ultach* and *An Guth*. She also writes reviews, academic and journalistic articles in *The Irish Times, Comhar*, and *Taighde agus Teagasc* and others.

Nuala Ní Chonchúir is a short story writer, novelist and poet, born in Dublin and living in Ballinasloe. Her third poetry collection *The Juno Charm* is just out from Salmon Poetry. Her fourth short story collection *Mother America* was published by New Island in May 2012. Nuala's story *'Peach'*, in the current issue of Prairie Schooner, has been nominated for the 2012 Pushcart Prize.
www.nualanichonchuir.com

Eiléan Ní Chuilleanáin, born in 1942, is married to Macdara Woods; they have a son, Niall. With Leland Bardwell and Pearse Hutchinson, they are founder editors of the literary review Cyphers. She has published six collections of poetry; her awards include the Patrick Kavanagh Prize. Educated in Cork and Oxford, she is a Fellow of Trinity College Dublin, and a member of Aosdána.

Doireann Ní Ghríofa is as Co an Chláir. Bhain sí amach céim mháistreachta sa Nua-Ghaeilge. Tá filíocht léi foilsithe i bhFeasta, Comhar, *Prairie Schooner* (Contemporary Irish Writers Issue), *Cyphers, Ropes Anthology, Revival, An tUltach, Crannóg, The Stony Thursday Book agus An Gael*. Beidh tuilleadh dánta á fhoilsiú go luath i Melusine. Bhain sí duais amach san Oireachtais Liteartha 2010 i rannóg na Scríbhneoirí Úra agus bhí dán léi ar ghearrliosta *Comórtas Uí Néill*

2011. Bhronn an Chomhairle Ealaíon sparánacht uirthi. D'fhoilsigh Coiscéim an chéad cnuasach léi, dár dteideal Résheoid, agus foilseofar a dara chnuasach Dúlasair i 2012.

Eibhlín Nic Eochaidh was born in Bray, County Wicklow and lives in Glenfarne, County Leitrim. A sometime clerical worker, shop assistant, gardener and guide, she won the Patrick Kavanagh Award and the Samhain Award for the translation of a poem into Irish.

Gearoid O'Brien was born in 1955 and is a native of Athlone. He has been writing poetry and prose for over thirty-five years and is widely published. He is the author of over a dozen books on aspects of his native town and county. His poems have appeared in Neptune's Kingdom, Prospice and Poetry Ireland Review and he has frequently contributed to Sunday Miscellany. In recent times he has poems published in *Abridged* (Derry) and Revival (Galway). He is a librarian in his native Athlone and is married to writer and theologian, Angela Hanley, and has two adult children

Paul Ó Colmáin lives and works in West Cork, Ireland. He was a winner of the inaugural Poet's Podium, 1995 run by Samhlaíocht Chiarraí and is a regular contributor of poems in both Irish and English to journals and anthologies. He is a musician, songwriter, visual artist and tour guide. http://www.paulocolmain.com

Gréagóir Ó Dúill is a bilingual poet, long associated with the Poets' House, Falcarragh, his selected verse in Irish, *Annála,* was published by Comhar in December 2011. Doghouse published *Outward and Return* in summer 2012.

Michael O'Flanagan is the editor of the poetry broadsheet Riposte, which was launched in 1996 and which now has members in Ireland, England, Germany, France, Italy, Belgium, America, Canada, Korea and Malta. A member of the Inchicore Writers' Group, Syllables, he is a former editor of The Inchicore Times and secretary of The Francis Ledwidge Society. He has published three collections of his poetry. He has broadcast his poetry on several local radio stations in the Dublin area and much of his work has also been included in the Syllables anthologies.
http://gofree.indigo.ie/~riposte/

Donal O'Flynn comes from Charleville, Co. Cork. He has been a regular attendee at poetry workshops and readings, and been published in numerous anthologies and journals. He is the author of two poetry collections published by Revival Press *"Lost Grace"* and *"The Tailor and Ansty Poem."* When in Ireland - he is a regular attendee at the open-mic poetry sessions, at the White House Bar, and 'On The Nail', Limerick.

Liam O'Meara is a poet and author from Dublin. His latest publication *The Life and Works of Michael Moran*, includes much previously unknown material about Dublin's most famous beggar poet of the 19th century. Liam has also written a number of books about various aspects of the Liberties and the poetry of Irish war poet, Francis Ledwidge.

Ciarán O' Rourke is *twenty years old,* and lives in Dublin. His poems have appeared in a number of publications, including *Poetry Review, The*

Spectator, New Welsh Review, The Irish Times, The Shop, The Moth and others. In 2009 he was winner of the Lena Maguire/Cúirt New Irish Writing award at the Cúirt International Festival of Literature. His pocket-pamphlet *Some Poems* was published as a Moth Edition in 2011

Dónal O' Siodhachain was born in the heart of the Sliabh Luachra. A regular of the White House Poetry group in Limerick. Donal was a post graduate history student in Mary Immaculate College- University of Limerick. He died in October 2012.

Derry O'Sullivan is a former student of Seán Ó Tuama, his poetry collections in Irish are *Cá bhfuil do Iudás?* (Dublin, Coscéim, 1987) winner of four Oireachtas poetry awards and the Sean O Riordáin Memorial Prize; *Cá bhfuil Tiarna Talún l'Univers?* (Coscéim, 1994); and *An Lá go dTáinig Siad*, Coscéim, 2005. His own work appears in translation in *The King's English* (Paris, First Impressions, 1987); and *En Mal de Fleurs* (Québec, Lèvres Urbaines, 1988), a suite of poems written directly in French. A former Catholic priest, he teaches at the Sorbonne, the Institut Catholique and the Institut Supèrieur d'Eléctronique de Paris. He lives in Paris.

John Pinschmidt is a retired American high school English teacher, living in Herbertstown, Co. Limerick with his Irish wife. He was first runner up in Limerick's *2009 Cuisle International Poetry Slam,* and has had poems published in the *Revival Literary Journal , Thefirstcut*, the *Open Mouse* site of *Poetry Scotland, Boyne Berries 10, Stony Thursday Book 10, Poetic Humour* (Whitehouse Bar Poets) and in *The Clare Champion*. He is one of six poets in Revival's Sextet, published in December, 2010, and is part of the Poetry Plus Writers' Group sponsored by the Limerick Writers' Centre.

Mark Roper has published 6 poetry collections, most recently *A Gather of A Shadow* Dedalus Press, 2012. The River Book, a collaboration with photographer Paddy Dwan, was published in 2010.

Dr Robyn Rowland AO has published nine books, six of poetry, most recently *Seasons of doubt & burning. New & Selected Poems* (2010) representing 40 years of poetry. Her poetry has recently appeared in *Being Human, ed. Neil Astley,* (Bloodaxe Books, UK, 2011). *Silence & its tongues* (2006) was shortlisted for the 2007 ACT Judith Wright Poetry Prize. Robyn is winner of poetry prizes, including the Writing Spirit Poetry Award, Ireland 2010. Robyn has created two CD's: *Off the tongue* and *Silver Leaving - Poems & Harp* with Irish harpist Lynn Saoirse. She has read her poetry in Portugal, Ireland, UK, USA, Greece, India, Austria, Bosnia, Serbia, Turkey & Italy, where, along with Canada, Spain and Japan she has been published. She is an Honorary Fellow, School of Culture and Communication, University of Melbourne, Australia. Robyn curates and presents the Poetry & Conversation Series for the Geelong Library Corporation.

Carol Rumens is the author of fifteen collections of poems, among them *Poems, 1968-2004* (Bloodaxe Books), *Blind Spots* (Seren, 2008) and *De Chirico's Threads* (Seren, 2010). She has published occasional fiction, including a novel, *Plato Park* (Chatto, 1987) and had several plays produced. She has received the Cholmondeley Award and the Prudence

Farmer Prize, and was joint recipient with Thomas McCarthy of an Alice Hunt Bartlett Award. She was Director of the Philip Larkin Centre for Poetry and Creative Writing at the University of Hull between 2005-6, and is now a part-time Professor of Creative Writing at the University of Bangor and Visiting Professor of Creative Writing at the University of Hull. She is currently a judge of the Eric Gregory Awards, and contributes a regular blog, Poem of the Week, to the Guardian Books Online. She is a Fellow of the Royal Society of Literature.

John W. Sexton was born in 1958. He is the author of four collections of poetry, *The Prince's Brief Career,* Foreword by Nuala Ní Dhomhnaill, (Cairn Mountain Press, 1995), *Shadows Bloom / Scáthanna Faoi Bhláth,* a book of haiku with translations into Irish by Gabriel Rosenstock, *Vortex* (Doghouse, 2005), and *Petit Mal* (Revival Press, 2009). A fifth collection, *The Offspring of the Moon,* is due from Salmon Poetry during Summer 2013.

He has been nominated for The Hennessy Literary Award and his poem "The Green Owl" won the Listowel Poetry Prize 2007 for best single poem. He was awarded a Patrick And Katherine Kavanagh Fellowship In Poetry for 2007/2008. He is one of the most requested writers currently working under Poetry Ireland's Writers-In-Schools Scheme.

Valerie Sirr holds an M.Phil in Creative Writing from Trinity College, Dublin, and her fiction and flash fiction have been widely published as well as some poetry. Awards include the 2007 Hennessy New Irish Writer Award, two Arts Council of Ireland bursaries and other literary prizes. She teaches creative writing and literature appreciation and has facilitated writing workshops for Dublin Simon Community and other groups in the community. She has completed a collection of short stories.
She blogs at www.valeriesirr.wordpress.com

Aaron Smith is a 27 year old PhD student at Queen's University Belfast. Originally from Portadown Co.Armagh. Aaron's current research area is the 'poetics of repetition and traumatic style in British poetry from 1936 to 1946'. He previously undertook a study of poet Robert Graves for his M.A thesis.

Gerard Smyth was born in Dublin where he still lives. His poetry has appeared widely in publications in Ireland, Britain, and America, as well as in translation, since the late 1960s. He is the author of seven collections, the most recent of which is *The Fullness of Time, New and Selected Poems* (Dedalus Press, 2010). He is a member of Áosdana.

Martin Vaughan is a civil servant living in Dublin. He is a founding member of the Irish Haiku Society and his haiku and poetry have appeared in a number of publications and online journals.

Mark Whelan is native of Limerick City where he still lives. He holds a BA Degree in Philosophy, English and Religious Studies. His publications include *Scarecrow Diptych* (Anam Press, 2002); *Always Pushing the Pull Door* (Revival Press, 2007) and *Brighton Suite* (Pighog Press, 2010). His collection, *The Sear of Wounds,* was published by DOGHOUSE Books in 2012.

Macdara Woods was born in 1942 and is married to Eiléan Ní Chuilleanáin; they have a son, Niall. With Leland Bardwell and Pearse Hutchinson, they are founder editors of the literary review *Cyphers*. He has published ten books of poems, translated from a number of languages and edited *The Kilkenny Anthology*. He has travelled widely, but now lives mostly in Dublin. He is a member of Aosdána.

Augustus Young was born in Cork, Ireland, in 1943, and now lives in a port town on the border between France and Spain. His most recent publications are *Diversifications: Poems and Translations* (Shearsman, 2009), and *The Nicotine Cat and Other People: Chronicles of the Self* (New Island/ Duras, 2009). He has published innumerable books of poetry and is widely anthologised. His regular webzine is www.augustusyoung.com.

Photographer

Laura Jean Zito is a Harvard University honours graduate who has worked for a number of years as a photographer for NBC Network News, NYC, and as unit still photographer on feature films such as *Breakin*. She is published in numerous books and magazines including *Cultural Survival Quarterly* and *National Geographic*. Ms. Zito is the first American woman to win the grand prize in the Nikon Photography Contest International (NPCI). She is currently working on a book about the Sinai tribe. She lives between New York and Ireland.

Editor

James Lawlor was born in Limerick in 1986 and is a graduate of the University of Limerick and the Queen's University of Belfast. At the University of Limerick he read English Literature and Media Studies. In 2010 he completed a M.A in English Literature (majoring in Irish Writing) at the Queen's University Belfast. His M.A thesis was entitled 'Are these my people?'; A Study of Contemporary Working-Class Writers. A Hartnett scholar, he has undertaken a number of studies on Michael Hartnett's poetry and is on the organising committee of Éigse Michael Hartnett Literary and Arts Festival. He is editor of the Michael Hartnett website (www.Michael-Hartnett.com) a website he designed as an undergraduate to promote the work of the poet. James has organised and taught a number of writing outreach workshops for the Frank McCourt Museum and the County Limerick Arts Office. He has produced a number of documentaries for radio and is currently working as an assistant in the Department of the Taoiseach. www.JamesLawlor.ie